Praise for

Better Than Vegan

"*Better Than Vegan* is the Holy Grail of human diets.
Read, learn, and thrive."

> —**Howard Lyman, author,**
> *Mad Cowboy and No More Bull!*

"Chef Del has battled his own dietary demons and
emerged triumphant. His deliciously healthy recipes
are victories for all of us who care about eating well."

> —**Rory Freedman, coauthor,** *Skinny Bitch*

"Chef Del has just expanded your repertoire of healthy
hearty delicious dishes. His creative instructions on
cooking without animals or oils will move you quickly
along to a better life."

> —**Dr. John McDougall, MD, and Mary McDougall,**
> **creators of the McDougall Program, and**
> **bestselling authors of** *The Starch Solution*

"The key to achieving optimum health is getting the right food onto your plate. *Better Than Vegan* could help you do that!"

—Alona Pulde, MD, and Matthew Lederman, MD

"After Chef Del offers his very relatable, fascinating story of struggle with his weight, he valiantly swoops in with the ultimate solution—a low fat, whole food, plant-based diet. I highly recommend this book as you will fall in love both with the magnificent and healthy recipes as well as their charming creator."

—Julieanna Hever, MS, RD, CPT, author of
The Complete Idiot's Guide to Plant-Based Nutrition
and host of What Would Julieanna Do?

"As Chef Del Sroufe points out, health doesn't come from a 'vegan' diet, it comes from a 'whole food, plant-based' diet. The recipes are simple enough, and yet a collection of delicious yet truly healthful options. This is a vegan cookbook that I can wholeheartedly endorse for my patients."

—Dr. Heather Shenkman, cardiologist

Better Than Vegan

Gado Gado (page 202)

Chef Del's
Better
Than
Vegan

**101 Favorite Low-Fat, Plant-Based Recipes
That Helped Me Lose Over 200 Pounds**

Del Sroufe

New York Times bestselling author of *Forks Over Knives—The Cookbook*
and Co-Owner and Chef for Wellness Forum Foods

with Glen Merzer

Foreword by Lindsay S. Nixon

BenBella Books • Dallas, TX

BenBella

BenBella Books, Inc.
10300 N. Central Expressway, Suite 530
Dallas, TX 75231
www.benbellabooks.com

Send feedback to feedback@benbellabooks.com

Printed in the United States of America

10 9 8 7 6 5 4 3 2 1

Library of Congress Cataloging-in-Publication Data
is available for this title.
978-1-939529-42-8

Editing by Vy Tran
Copyediting by Shannon Kelly and Nicole Schlosser
Proofreading by Jennifer Greenstein and Lisa Story
Indexing by Marilyn Flaig
Recipe and author photographs by Robert Metzger
Process and ingredient photographs by Adam Koch
Cover design by Ty Nowicki
Text design and composition by Ralph Fowler / rlfdesign
Printed by Versa Press, Inc.

Distributed by Perseus Distribution
(www.perseusdistribution.com)

To place orders through Perseus Distribution:
Tel.: (800) 343-4499
Fax: (800) 351-5073
E-mail: orderentry@perseusbooks.com

Significant discounts for bulk sales are available. Please contact Glenn Yeffeth at
glenn@benbellabooks.com or (214) 750-3628.

I dedicate this book to my parents, who loved me, fed me, clothed me, gave me shelter, educated me, and wanted me to be.

Spinach-Artichoke Dip (page 141)

Contents

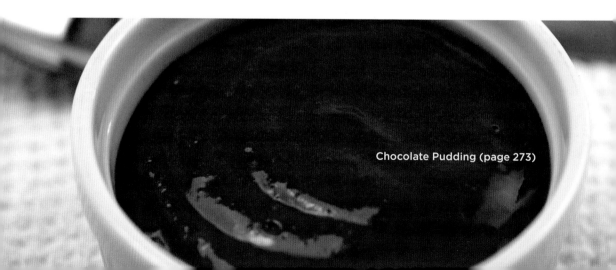

Chocolate Pudding (page 273)

White Bean Pesto (page 138)

Foreword

I met Del at a vegan chili-off in Texas. We were both "celebrity judges" and bonded over the fact that neither of us actually liked chili. Oops. (Side note: You know the winner truly won because Del and I had three helpings each of the winning chili!)

Before meeting Del in person, however, I'd long heard about his work at the Wellness Forum. Although there is no shortage of chefs in the culinary world, there aren't many who cook like I do: using plant-based, whole foods and no oil. But Del does!

Del understands that you don't need fat and frying for flavor and that wholesome, healthy food can be delicious. His recipes also show how sophisticated plant-based cooking can be. "Gourmet" doesn't have to be synonymous with "unhealthy." Eating well can be both elegant and part of your everyday meals, not just special occasions.

Perhaps Del understands this better than anyone. Unlike me, Del's culinary career didn't start when he adopted a healthier diet. Rather, his career has been shaped by it. Del began cooking in a vegetarian kitchen, but the food was your average restaurant fare, full of oil. Then he opened a vegan bakery with vegan treats that rivaled their non-vegan counterparts in taste, but were not necessarily healthier.

Eventually, Del found himself in a bit of a health-care crisis and he changed his lifestyle—including the way he cooked and baked. Out went the oils and in came even more fresh foods—vegetables, grains, legumes, fruits, and limited nuts and seeds. Del found new ways to ramp up flavor and satisfaction but with health in mind. As a result, Del and his customers were happier and healthier—and with his help, you can be, too!

Del's personal story, which is also shared in this book, is awe-inspiring. All of us can find a bit of ourselves in Del's story and his continued journey to health.

—Lindsay S. Nixon

My Story

My Battle
with Food

I may be the luckiest guy I ever met.

A decade ago, I ate myself to 475 pounds—on a vegan diet. That's one heck of a lot of vegan pizzas, French fries, guacamole, fried vegetables, fried tofu, salads loaded with oily dressings, Thai coconut-curry stews, peanut butter, bread, muffins, pastries, donuts, pretzels, potato chips, cookies, oil-popped popcorn topped with melted margarine, dried fruits, nuts, chocolate bars, soy ice cream, coconut macaroons, and all kinds of cake, washed down with beer, wine, soda, and fruit juice.

While all of these foods can conform to a vegan diet, they're highly caloric. Eating them regularly can make almost anyone fat, even if it takes the rare individual like me, with the right combination of genes, compulsiveness, and appetite, to eat enough to reach 475 pounds.

The reason I consider myself so lucky is that I managed to attain such a massive weight without developing any form of heart disease or any chronic illnesses. I survived my decades-long descent into the abyss of morbid obesity and came out on the other side. I now weigh 230 pounds, still a little above my ideal weight but getting close to the proper weight for my six-foot-three frame.

The weight that I gained on a vegan diet I also lost on a vegan diet—needless to say, a much better vegan diet. There are plenty of good reasons to adopt the vegan lifestyle, ranging from spiritual beliefs to concerns about personal health and the well-being of the planet, but I'm living proof that, at least as far as health goes, simply avoiding animal products isn't good enough if you're eating the wrong foods. It's not enough just to be vegan. You've got to be better than that. You won't improve your health unless your diet is low in fat and high in whole, nutritious foods.

I'm a native of Columbus, Ohio, where I have a few generations of roots and a lot of family and friends. So isolation and loneliness did not bring on my morbid obesity. But a growing degree of isolation and loneliness was the inevitable consequence.

The weight gain started when I was six, after my parents' divorce. For a short period of time, as my parents were splitting up, my mother, brothers, and I lived with my maternal grandmother, who on a typical day would serve large portions of corned beef and cabbage, always insisting that I eat my plate clean so nothing would go to waste.

Once we moved out of my grandmother's house, my mom ruled the kitchen again. Mom loved to cook, and sometimes she'd knock herself out and come up with something special like duck *à l'orange* with a Grand Marnier sauce. Occasionally, she would get eclectic: she once made deer brains with scrambled eggs. I thought that was a pretty good meal, although the deer probably didn't.

More often, she would cook simple meals like fried chicken or pork chops or meatloaf with a salad or a vegetable. Or my least favorite staple of her repertoire: a poached egg atop a bed of spinach. But she did have some delicious specialties, such as pumpkin bread, pound cake, and rum balls made from vanilla wafers, butter, sugar, cocoa, and rum. When I was a teenager, she once baked a couple dozen rum balls as a present for a friend, set them in their cookie tin on the kitchen table, and made the mistake of leaving the room. I ate

every last one before she returned. Boy, that made her mad, but, to be fair, she was the one who left the room.

My father, now a retired federal judge, was one of nine siblings. He came from a family of farmers, and when there was a meal on the Sroufe family farm (my grandparents' farm) in southern Ohio, it would often be an extravagant, multicourse meal, especially on holidays. My paternal grandmother and her daughters, my aunts, were very much Southern cooks. So when we visited her farm, there would be fried chicken or ham or roast beef, mashed potatoes and gravy, green beans cooked with ham hocks and sugar, or scalloped oysters. My father sometimes contributed by making something called "blood pudding"; I could probably find out what was in it by Googling the term, but I'm not yet that brave. Much of the food at these gatherings was fried and lots of it was lathered with rich sauces. Eating "healthy" in my family meant eating chicken without the skin.

There was always plenty of fat and meat in every meal. And then there were the desserts. My favorite was transparent pie, made from eggs, butter, evaporated milk, sugar, and vanilla. It was a truly rich and greasy treat—pure heaven.

It may not shock you to learn that most members of the family were overweight.

I had other favorite foods as a kid, some of them quite simple. I loved to make fried egg and ketchup sandwiches. I would also put sugar on white bread, believe it or not, and wolf it down. I could easily eat half a loaf of white bread with sugar on it in one sitting. Or cinnamon toast: I'd put butter, sugar, and cinnamon on white bread and toast it in the toaster oven to a delicious brown.

Having grown up eating fatty, sweet, nutritionally vacant foods like that, it's not surprising that I've struggled with my weight all my life. I was but eight years old, and my brother Jeffrey only six, when a doctor put us on a calorie-restrictive diet—800 calories per day. During that period, we would go to that doctor for weekly weigh-ins, which I dreaded. I always got jealous when Jeffrey lost more weight than I did. After a while, the family gave up on the tedious weigh-ins, and I was grateful for that.

I was always the biggest kid in the class both in terms of height and weight. In tenth grade, I joined the marching band. I wore the biggest uniform that the school had for marching band, and man, was it tight on me. All I can say is I think that uniform might have helped me hit the high notes on my alto sax.

Although my older brother Tony, who didn't suffer the weight problem that Jeffrey and I did, called me "fatso" for most of my life, I rarely took verbal abuse for my weight from anyone else. It's pretty strange, when I think about it, how infrequently the subject of my weight came up in conversation. The fatter I got, the more off-limits the subject became. I think people were embarrassed by my weight, and even those who cared about me the most rarely broached the subject. I would be the biggest person in the room, but I often felt invisible, which I guess was fine by me. My mother

would claim that I slouched when I walked in order to try to make myself less noticeable.

There were precious few periods of my life when I was fit. In my first year of college, I got myself down to 216 pounds. But I partied and drank way too much during the remaining years of college and didn't stay in shape. In 1989, at the age of twenty-nine, I briefly returned to the weight I had achieved as a freshman. But from the time I was thirty years old until my late forties, my weight fluctuated constantly but never dipped under 280 pounds. And in my midforties I hit my lamentable personal high of 475.

My father was instrumental in getting me to stop drinking to excess. Like a stern judge, he laid down the law on that one. But no family member or friend ever made a direct effort to stop my eating to excess. To be fair, I suppose my father tried, in his own diplomatic way: when my brother Jeffrey and I were both in the 400-pound range, Dad made a comment like, "You know, Del, I'm getting a little concerned about your brother's weight." I remember my grandfather would tell me not to eat so fast or not to put such big bites in my mouth, but no relative or friend told me I was eating too much, and certainly nobody told me I was eating the wrong types of foods, since I was basically eating the same sorts of foods that they were eating. It just wasn't acceptable in my family to criticize or comment upon a person's intake of food. Besides, I don't think they would have known what to say. Plenty of my family members had weight problems of their own, if not as severe as mine.

I remember the first time I learned that I was over 300 pounds. I was in a Sears department store. With trepidation, I stepped on a scale and discovered that I was 313 pounds. I was shocked. I never dreamt that I would exceed 300 pounds. Even though I had always seen myself as fat, I didn't think I was in the league with the 300-pounders. Most of the scales you buy for the home don't go over 250 or 275, so I hadn't realized the territory I had lapsed into. That was a wake-up call. Unfortunately, instead of propelling me to better health through a sustainable diet, that wake-up call sent me into a shell. I performed the daily tasks I was obligated to perform: I went to work or I went to school, and I came home. I avoided people. I starved myself, and then I binged.

The fatter I got, the more off-limits the subject became. I think people were embarrassed by my weight, and even those who cared about me the most rarely broached the subject.

In many ways, my life often revolved around the restrictions that my weight placed upon me. I stopped dancing, something I used to enjoy. I wouldn't go to the beach; I didn't want to take my shirt off. At 400 pounds, I stopped skiing; I couldn't steer myself. I stopped riding my bike. For long stretches of time, I didn't date; I didn't want anyone touching me. I didn't go out to eat often because I was sensitive about how others would look at me when I ordered or when my food arrived. I could sense them judging me by how I ate, trying to discern what exactly my eating problem was. In public, there-fore, I tried to be a healthy eater. I wanted it to appear as if my eating pattern wasn't the problem. So I made healthy choices in public and did all my binging in private.

For a period of years, I effectively became a hermit. I remember a time when I put aside my anxieties and met a group of friends in Max & Erma's restaurant, a hamburger joint, sat on a chair, and fell right through it. Although I tried to laugh it off, I was filled with shame and embarrassment. It was pretty clear that it wasn't the chair's fault.

In 1989, I got a part-time job managing an offbeat vegetarian restaurant, the King Avenue Coffeehouse, for $5 an hour. I wound up staying at the job for eight and a half years. I became a good friend of the owner, and she spoke to me a lot about vegetarianism. In the course of my career at that restaurant, I naturally met plenty of vegetarians, vegans, raw foodists, and others with dietary lifestyles outside of the mainstream.

I looked into the issues that led people to make their dietary choices and became pretty disturbed about the way animals are treated for the sake of food production. So my introduction to vegetarianism had more to do with its ethical and spiritual dimensions than with health concerns.

After five or six years of working at the King Avenue Coffeehouse, I became a vegetarian myself. Yes, I guess it took a while for those ethical and spiritual considerations to overcome dietary tastes cultivated—if you could apply the term "cultivated" to a bent for the greasy foods to which I had grown accustomed—over a lifetime. But giving up meat was a natural transition for me, since I was living above the restaurant at that point and learning to cook vegetarian food on the job. Even so, I would cheat on my newfound vegetarianism when I'd go home for the holidays and have meals with my family. It would have been easier to escape noise at the Super Bowl than to escape animal-based foods in those meals. The holiday meals at home didn't change my commitment to my new diet, however. One of the last tasks I performed for the King Avenue Coffeehouse was serving as its pastry chef, and I adapted the restaurant's recipes to turn its entire pastry menu vegan. I was convinced by then that vegan was the way to go.

My next career move—opening my own vegan bakery, Del's Bread, in 1997—might have been the worst mistake I ever made with regard to combating my weight problem. Upon opening the bakery, I hit the panic mode, determined to do whatever was necessary to make the business survive. As a consequence, I gave up any effort to maintain my own health. Working eighty-hour weeks, I quit exercising and practicing self-care. I gave up the walking and bike riding that I used to do. I no longer planned my meals or paid any attention to what I considered a "balanced meal"—a potato, another vegetable, and a protein source, for example. I would eat scones for breakfast and whatever was in the pastry case for lunch, and would constantly eat whatever we were getting ready to throw out because it had gone stale. It was, after all, unacceptable to waste food. I was eating on the go, working while shoveling food in my mouth. I wasn't conscious of what I was eating; it was all about keeping the hunger away, indulging my appetite, and taste-testing my creations while remaining on my feet sometimes from five in the morning until nine at night. There was no time to make a salad or steamed vegetables. I would go home dog-tired, pass out, and then wake up and do it all again.

It would be years before I processed the lessons learned from my crazed bakery days into five basic rules of nutrition. Let's begin the countdown here with Chef Del's Fifth Law of Nutrition: *Working around the clock is not good for the waistline.* You need to devote sufficient time to take care of yourself, to exercise, and to eat healthy meals. However hard you need to work, allow enough time for those basics.

It was during the four overworked years when I owned and operated the bakery that I ate my way to

475 pounds. I gained close to 200 pounds on a strictly vegan diet.

That's quite an achievement, I know.

Owning and running a bakery was a lifestyle that required an enormous amount of energy, but it's hard to maintain your energy when you reach a weight that stratospheric. Going up and down the stairs became terribly hard on my knees. At least twice a day I had to stop whatever I was doing and lie down for about a half hour to get my energy back.

It's also hard, at that weight, to maintain your optimism and enthusiasm for life. Depression would overtake me and I'd sometimes, on off days, sleep for half

the day, not wanting to leave the house or see people or do things. Or I'd simply eat and drink and sit in front of the TV. I might eat a half gallon of soy ice cream or a dozen vegan donuts. My secret place to eat was in my car. That tradition had begun in my meat-eating days. Back then, I would go to the Souvlaki Palace on campus at Ohio State and order two gyros, two bags of French fries, and two large Cokes, and then wolf it all down while sitting in my 1971 Chevy Impala in the parking lot. Now I was doing the same with donuts and other vegan treats. I could practically eat myself into a coma. I was shoving my emotions back down my throat, and when I had enough to eat, I just wanted to sleep.

And so we come to Chef Del's Fourth Law of Nutrition: *Having a secret place to eat is generally a bad sign.*

And I dieted, of course. I resolved over and over again to defeat my demons and eat the right foods in the right proportions to create a new me. I tried all kinds of popular diets and I "invented" a few myself, adapting fad diets to my vegan proclivities. Yes, I even created my own vegan Atkins diet. I accepted the central premise of the Atkins Diet books—that fat and protein were the good macronutrients and carbohydrates were the problem—and I simply substituted high-protein plant foods, like tempeh and seitan, for the recommended meats and dairy in the Atkins program. Vegan buffalo wings became a staple food during that experiment.

Chef Del's Third Law of Nutrition: *You're in deep shit when vegan buffalo wings are a staple of your diet.*

My vegan Atkins diet didn't help me lose weight, but it did help me develop intense carbohydrate cravings and a bad case of constipation. Still, it was better than the all-you-can-eat cabbage soup diet, which was hell on a guy like me who loves variety. If I had one more bowl of cabbage soup during that penitential extravaganza, I might have needed to check myself into a padded room. I went through innumerable other diets, often involving caloric restriction. I would pour foods into measuring cups before putting them in a bowl.

Chef Del's Second Law of Nutrition: *Life is too short for pouring your cold cereal into a measuring cup before you put it in your bowl.*

The periods of caloric restriction followed by periods of binging always left me in worse shape than when I began. It was classic yo-yo dieting. The ride I was on might have been bumpy, but the long-term trajectory was always downhill. I was never satisfied with myself, and I wasn't enjoying my journey. I thought of myself as fat even when I lost considerable amounts of weight, and I hit new highs far more often than I hit new lows.

It couldn't have been good for my heart to be charged with the task of pumping blood to such an enormous body mass, but I never had a heart attack or developed angina or felt pressure in my chest. I never developed diabetes, hypertension, or cancer, to name just three diseases linked to obesity. I don't know how I managed to reach 475 pounds without suffering the

If I had one more bowl of cabbage soup during that penitential extravaganza, I might have needed to check myself into a padded room.

expected health consequences. I can only say to you, please, don't try this at home.

It's possible that a small degree of protection was conferred upon me because I got fat on plant foods rather than animal foods. It's possible that being a 475-pound vegan is just a touch less profoundly unhealthy than being a 475-pound meat eater. I can't say that for certain, and nobody's ever going to find out by doing a scientific study comparing the longevity of 475-pound

vegans to that of 475-pound meat eaters. There's no screaming need to resolve that issue with science. All I know for sure is that I was incredibly lucky to have attained such a debilitating state without doing permanent damage to myself.

The worst that happened was tearing a ligament in my foot and injuring my ankle one day in 2005 when I fell while walking on snow, carrying groceries into the house. It was a minor but excruciatingly painful injury. I knew that the tear might never have happened, or might not have been so severe, had my weight been normal. I tried to pop my foot back into place, limped into the house, took three ibuprofens, and lay down on the couch for an hour. Then I got up, wrapped the foot in a bandage, and went back to work. I was self-employed and I didn't have health insurance. I just coped with the pain, which remained severe for a long time. I kept the foot wrapped up for a couple of years and kept a stool in the kitchen to sit on so that I wouldn't have to be on my feet so much.

That nuisance of a foot-and-ankle injury is what led me in 2005 to Columbus's own Wellness Forum, where I met with its founder, my good friend Dr. Pam Popper, and told her I was ready to do whatever it takes to get healthy.

I had maintained a weight of over 400 pounds for the past four years. It was clear that I wasn't going to overcome my weight problem without help. Surrendering myself—if you can call it that—to the Wellness Forum was a hard thing for me to do because I'm not a group person. I'm not by nature and temperament a joiner. I consider myself an outgoing person; I like to be with friends—but informally, not in structured groups.

Still, I had tried often enough on my own to combat my weight problem and failed miserably. And I trusted Pam. We'd been introduced back in the 1980s by an old roommate of mine with whom she had gone to high school. We reconnected in 1999 when she came into my bakery and asked me to replicate a granola bar using healthy ingredients. I could tell she was a very driven person, very determined to make things happen. I developed an immediate respect for her as a business-person. And we had something of a parallel history in Columbus. We had both attended the same high school, though she's five years older than I am. My Aunt Joyce had been her eighth-grade English teacher. Columbus may not be a small town, but when you live there long enough, it can feel that way.

You're probably wondering exactly what the Well-ness Forum is. It's primarily an informational orga-nization; its central product is education. You pay a modest fee to become a member, and that entitles you to attend a ten-hour course on health and wellness, participate in cooking and nutrition classes, access members-only portions of the Web site, join conference calls on health-related subjects, and attend monthly dinners, in addition to receiving ongoing support and educational materials. People from all over the world join the Wellness Forum, but its headquarters is in Columbus.

People don't change until they're ready to change. I was clearly ready to change. I was overdue.

At the time I joined, the Wellness Forum headquarters was a two-room facility without a kitchen. I would do cooking demos on propane stovetops. People like me with weight and health issues would go there, determined to turn our lives around but daunted by the task, in much the same way alcoholics would straggle into an A.A. meeting. There's an ongoing stream of information given to you and there's a lot of support. You get calls from caring facilitators. And, as with A.A., you find that people don't change until they're ready to change. I was clearly ready to change. I was overdue. And I knew that the Wellness Forum's dietary protocol wasn't some thirty-day, quick-fix program to health. I knew it was designed to be a program for the rest of your life.

About a year after I joined the program, Pam asked me to partner with her in a new business, Wellness Forum Foods. We would have a meal delivery service and create foods for sale that were compliant with the diet we were promoting. I had already started my own meal delivery service after Del's Bread had folded, so my clients would become clients of Wellness Forum Foods, and most of the fat and all of the oil would now have to be removed from the meals that I was preparing for them.

Oil had been a fixture in most of those recipes. My one stipulation about removing oil, which I expressed to Pam, was that the food would still have to taste good. Health was important, sure, but I wasn't about to sacrifice taste on its altar, and thereby lose customers. As a chef, I was all about making meals tasty, so I naturally worried about encountering angry customers complaining of food that had lost its flavor. In that event, health would be no defense. I couldn't tell them to shut up and eat my creations because the grub was good for their arteries. Pam assured me that I could make the food taste just as good without the oil. Frankly, I was dubious.

Pam was right. The truth is that nobody ever missed the oil or noticed it was absent. I was a little shocked by that. The only comment I can recall hearing came from one customer who told me how pleased he was that my food didn't taste so greasy anymore. That experience taught me the mind-boggling secret about oil: it's ubiquitous in processed foods, it's in most recipes you read, it has a prominent place in practically every kitchen pantry, and yet *you don't miss it when it's gone*. It's 100 percent fat with no health benefits (nope, not even olive oil offers any protective benefits), and in most dishes it's utterly unnecessary.

Oil is there in the first place only because it's a cheap ingredient that, to the unsophisticated palate, makes food seem more satisfying. It doesn't usually add flavor; it just adds the comforting sensation of fat.

Let me add just a small disclaimer here to my statement about the expendability of oil. I have been able to simply leave out the oil, or replace it, in most dishes that I used to prepare with oil. But there are a few foods that I've had to simply give up because oil is required. I no longer eat French fries or potato chips. I've not yet

I gained more
than 200 pounds
on a vegan diet
swimming in oil,
and I lost more
than 200 pounds
on a vegan diet
without oil. I
think that tells
you something.

been able to create a hash brown dish that works well without oil, and I've never been satisfied with any oil-free French toast. With those few exceptions, I can say that very few sacrifices are necessary to accommodate an oil-free cuisine.

Once you get used to cooking and eating without oil, you *do* notice it when you dine out and it's present. Once your tastes have changed, you find that oil adds an unpleasant greasiness to meals that would have been better without it. You can feel it in your throat, coating it like a pan.

You will find not a drop of oil in any of the recipes in this book, and I would encourage you to cook without it. Eliminating oil is a central tenet of a diet that's *Better Than Vegan.* The recipes in this book are all not merely vegan; they are all low-fat, whole-food vegan. After all, I gained more than 200 pounds on a vegan diet swimming in oil, and I lost more than 200 pounds on a vegan diet without oil. I think that tells you something.

Many factors contributed to my recovery, but the most important was developing an understanding of what foods to eat and how to prepare them to make them delicious and satisfying.

Which brings me, finally, to Chef Del's First Law of Nutrition: *It's gotta taste good.*

Diet Is a
Noun, Too

When I think about the verb "diet," I get uncomfortable. Call it a reflex by now. It brings up unpleasant memories for me, going back all the way to childhood, of caloric restriction. It brings up memories of the unwise choices I consistently made after periods of caloric deprivation, memories of splurging and purging. I don't want to go there anymore; I want instead to embrace "diet" as a noun, meaning sustenance, the daily fare, the stuff we should be eating. Once we understand "diet" as a noun and its role in health, we can assign the verb "diet" to the dustbin of history.

When we eat foods of the right kind, they fuel our cells efficiently, protect us from disease, keep us at (or nudge us toward) our optimal weight, and provide health-giving benefits in ways that science has only begun to understand. When we eat the wrong foods, they fuel our cells inefficiently, stress our organs,

leach minerals from our bones, clog our arteries, fog our brains, bring on disease, make us fat, addict us to nutritionally vacant substances, and provide no protective health benefits. It may sound simplistic, but food choices really are divided into good and bad (and, okay, some that may fall in-between because they contain both healthy and unhealthy ingredients). With exceptions for people with food allergies or intolerance of a substance like gluten, the same rules apply to all of us. We all have to avoid particular foods that we have trouble digesting or that cause adverse reactions. And we can all choose to emphasize those specific healthy foods that we most enjoy eating.

What to Avoid

Let's look at the ten dietary mistakes that we all need to watch out for, the first seven being sins of excess and the last three sins of deficiency:

1. Excessive fat of any sort

2. Excessive saturated fat

3. Excessive protein, especially animal protein

4. Cholesterol

5. Excessive flours

6. Overly processed foods

7. Concentrated sugars

8. Insufficient fiber

9. Insufficient water intake

10. Insufficient phytochemical intake

Let's review each of these mistakes one by one.

1. Excessive fat

Excessive fat includes fat from oils, margarine, coconut, chocolate, avocado, and nuts. Excessive fat is the leading cause of obesity and type 2 diabetes in America, and it contributes to heart disease and cancer as well. The optimal amount of calories as fat in one's diet is around 15 percent, but most Americans eat a diet

If you had to sum up in a couple of words what's most wrong with the American diet, what lies behind the epidemics of obesity, heart disease, diabetes, and cancer, "excessive fat" would probably be the best answer.

with calories-as-fat content in the range of 30 to 40 percent. There are nine calories in a gram of fat, while only four in a gram of carbohydrate or protein. If you had to sum up in a couple of words what's most wrong with the American diet, what lies behind the epidemics of obesity, heart disease, diabetes, and cancer, "excessive fat" would probably be the best answer. Some fats are better than others (the fat in nuts and seeds is preferable to the fats in oil, butter, and margarine, for example), but once the overall proportion of fat in the diet is too high, every fat calorie you consume is doing you damage. Yes, you really can eat too many avocados.

2. Excessive saturated fat

Saturated fat is the most dangerous form of fat because it clogs the arteries. Some of the foods that are highest in saturated fat are meat, chicken, fish, dairy, oils, coconut, and chocolate. There's no need for saturated fat in the human diet.

3. Excessive protein

The American diet is also plagued by excessive protein. Consuming protein in excess does us no good because the body cannot store protein. In fact, the need to excrete excess protein takes a toll on the kidneys and contributes to osteoporosis. The worst form of protein, contrary to popular myth, is actually animal protein because it's highly sulfuric. Dr. T. Colin Campbell did the groundbreaking work that demonstrated that animal protein, especially when consumed in excessive proportion in the diet, is actually carcinogenic; for a fuller explanation, read his book *The China Study.* The optimal range of calories as protein is 5 to 10 percent. Human breast milk, consumed during the period of greatest growth in our lives, and therefore the time when we have the greatest need for protein, is about 5 percent protein.

4. Cholesterol

There is no need for dietary cholesterol, period. The body manufactures all the cholesterol it needs in the liver. High cholesterol has of course been linked to heart disease, and whether it's simply a marker or a causative agent, it's also been linked to kidney and liver diseases, erectile dysfunction, and Alzheimer's disease. The optimal amount of dietary cholesterol is zero.

5. Excessive Flours

Excessive intake of foods made with flour is not helpful. That was certainly one of the causes of my explosive weight gain on a vegan diet. Flours are broken grains; they are concentrated calories. They fall under the category of "processed foods," though some flours are more processed than others. Whole-grain flour is preferable to white or refined flour, but you don't want to overdo consumption of flours in general, especially if you are trying to lose weight.

6. Overly processed foods

That brings us to processed foods in general. By "processed foods," I'm referring to foods that generally come in boxes or cans or jars in a grocery store, with long lists of ingredients, as opposed to whole foods that you purchase in the produce aisle or in the bulk section of grocery stores. If the ingredients are themselves refined or flavored or chemically altered, so much the worse. And it's no bargain if the manufactured food, or "food product," is also fortified with vitamins and minerals. Now I realize that you're probably not going to absolutely eliminate all processed foods from your diet; I've got to admit that I haven't completely eliminated them from my own. But the goal is to minimize our intake of processed foods, while maximizing our intake of low-fat, whole foods.

Another goal, which we will elaborate upon in the section on shopping, is to choose wisely when selecting the few processed foods that we allow in our diet. Keep in mind that the concept of processed food is elastic: tofu may be considered a processed food, but it's only lightly processed, made by boiling soybeans and separating the curd with a coagulating agent such as *nigari.* Margarine, by contrast, is a highly processed food. What we need to look out for in processed foods is added fat and sweeteners—vegetable oil and corn syrup, for example. Most processed foods will contain unnecessary fat and sweeteners because they are cheap for the manufacturer and satisfying to the consumer. Even tomato sauce, which can certainly be made delicious and serve its purpose ably without oil or sweeteners, will usually contain both. In general, a long list of ingredients is usually a tip-off to an overly processed food, as are individual ingredients that sound like they belong on a chemistry quiz. I would also caution against consuming any processed food containing any animal-based ingredient, such as whey.

[A] long list of ingredients is usually a tip-off to an overly processed food, as are individual ingredients that sound like they belong on a chemistry quiz.

7. Concentrated sugars

Concentrated sugars represent one of the deadliest dietary sins in America. They are addictive and appeal to the taste buds of most of us. We are not talking here about the natural sugar that comes in whole fruits. Concentrated sugars come in an abundance of forms: white sugar, brown sugar, evaporated cane juice, agave nectar, honey, maple syrup, molasses, fruit juice, high-fructose corn syrup, barley malt—the list goes on and on. They contribute to heart disease, diabetes, cancer, and obesity, and are ever present in processed foods. In my experience, this is probably the toughest food addiction to overcome; it has even been compared to cocaine addiction. But once you down-regulate your taste buds by staying away from sweetened food for a time, you will find that you have less interest in eating sugary desserts. You'll find, for example, that fresh pineapple will taste better than ever because sugar is no longer numbing your taste buds.

You can also, with a little effort, down-regulate your taste buds by staying away from fatty foods for a time. Eat a plain baked potato daily for a few days, seasoned just with salt and pepper. Learn to love it without the added fat. If you first learn to appreciate the natural joy of eating simple foods, then the flavors inherent in the recipes in this book will be all the more puissant for you. And I say that as a man who has never used the word "puissant" before, but has recently become a best-selling author.

Now to the sins of insufficiency . . .

8. Insufficient fiber

Fiber does us a world of good, from preventing constipation to escorting cholesterol and toxins out of the system. Science seems to learn more and more about the benefits of a high-fiber diet every year. The Standard American Diet is markedly low in fiber. You should be getting fiber with every meal.

9. Insufficient water intake

Many Americans suffer from dehydration and don't know it. If you're thirsty, you're likely already dehydrated. We have to drink a lot of water to hydrate our cells, burn calories efficiently, maintain a healthy blood volume, and flush toxins out our system. Fiber and water work in tandem to prevent constipation. I try to drink three or four quarts of water per day. It's not always easy.

10. Insufficient phytochemicals

Phytochemicals in foods are responsible for their color, and those bright colors are what would have attracted our ancestors to eat them. We know that phytochemicals protect plants from the elements, and so it's logical that they will protect us as well.

Phytochemicals protect us from cancer and other afflictions in ways that science only partially understands. Every year a little more is added to our collective body of knowledge about how chemicals found in plants interact to enhance our well-being. But this is an area where, when making dietary choices, logic and intuition come into play as much as science. There are an estimated 10,000 or more phytochemicals in food. They are all in plant foods, not animal foods. Some 4,000 or so phytochemicals have thus far been identified. Less than 10 percent of those have been studied in depth. Evidence suggests—if rarely proves outright—specific health benefits of individual phytochemicals.

Here are a handful of examples of power-packed phyto-chemicals:

- **Anthocyanins**, found in grapes, blueberries, and raspberries, are linked with anti-inflammatory and cancer-fighting properties; they are believed to protect the endothelial cells that line the blood vessels and to protect blood vessels from oxidative damage.

- **Resveratrol** in grapes, blueberries, and pomegranates may boost metabolism, lower blood sugar, and protect the nervous and cardiovascular systems.

- **Flavonoids**, found in all manner of plant foods, such as green tea, onions, beans, spinach, and strawberries, have a wide variety of health benefits, including antiviral, antibacterial, and anti-allergenic properties. Flavonoids also appear to suppress LDL cholesterol oxidation and inflammation in the artery walls, and to help prevent blood clots. One particular flavonoid, quercetin, found in citrus fruits, apples, onions, and parsley, may help prevent ulcers as well as cancer, and may also protect the prostate.

- **Sulfides** in garlic and onion may well boost the immune system.

- **Beta-carotene** and carotenoids in leafy greens and red, orange, and yellow fruits and vegetables offer protection against cancer, heart disease, macular degeneration, and cataracts.

The list goes on and on.

To definitely prove by scientific study the precise health benefits of individual phytochemicals is not an easy task. Try to imagine the difficulty of establishing as fact, for example, the proposition that sulfides in onions boost the human immune system. You can isolate the sulfides and put them in a pill and give them to study participants, but the sulfides may be designed by nature to work not alone but rather in harmony with dozens of other phytochemicals found in onions and in other

foods as well. In other words, if the benefits of sulfides are synergistic, they can't be replicated by isolating the substance in pill form. Instead of isolating the sulfides, you can instead try to design a study in which participants eat an onion a day, but you then have to control all other aspects of the participants' diets and compare their outcomes to those eating the exact same diet without onions, while controlling all other variables—a more or less impossible task. And any test designed to show a significant effect on the immune system would have to last a long period of time, not just a few weeks. Even then, you'd theoretically only be determining the healthfulness of onions, not necessarily sulfides. You can do a test on animals, but you will always run up against the argument that animal testing proves nothing definitive about human health, not to mention the moral arguments against animal experimentation.

So we have to be patient with science. But while we await more scientific data, we can take note of scientific patterns. And all the science points in the same direction: phytochemicals, obtained in whole foods, are good for you. They are the natural antidote to oxidative stress. It's been definitively proven that people who eat more fruits and vegetables have better health outcomes; they are less likely to suffer from cancer and heart disease. Phytochemicals are certainly part of the explanation, along with fiber. The best way to get an array of phytochemicals in your diet is to make sure you eat at least one big salad daily with a variety of greens and vegetables, and eat a few fruits every day, too.

Eat foods vibrant with color and you obtain a world of phytochemicals that go to work for you, whether or not you know the names science has bestowed on them and whether or not science knows exactly how they work.

If you instead try to obtain your phytochemicals in a pill, keep in mind that there is no real evidence of the efficacy of supplementation, and there is the risk of toxicity from unnaturally high doses of isolated chemicals.

Okay, now let's apply this basic understanding of nutritional principles to some potential food choices.

Let's start with flesh foods: a 3-ounce serving of beef, turkey, pork, chicken, or fish. (Keep in mind that people have been known to eat more than 3 ounces at a time.) It doesn't matter whether it's beef, turkey, pork, chicken, or fish; either way, your 3-ounce serving is going to contain between 3 and 7 grams of saturated fat. Between 50 and 80 percent of its overall calories are going to come from fat (and that's if there's no added fat in the cooking, like butter or oil); the remainder will be protein, since there's no carbohydrate in flesh foods. The calorie count (again, not including added calories from added fat in cooking oil or sauces) will be in the range of 180 to 250, and there will be about 60 to 90 mg of cholesterol. And that's for a small 3-ounce serving.

Now let's review how these flesh foods stack up against our dietary objectives. We're trying to practice a diet in which about 15 percent of our calories come from fat, but flesh foods are in the 50 to 80 percent category. We're trying to avoid saturated fat, but flesh

foods are extremely high in saturated fat. We're trying to limit our protein intake to about 5 to 10 percent of calories, but flesh foods are in the 20 to 50 percent range, and it's all animal protein, the most dangerous type. We're trying to avoid dietary cholesterol, but they're full of it. We're trying to obtain a lot of fiber, but there's no fiber in any animal food. And we want to take in phytochemicals to ward off disease, but there are no phytochemicals in animal foods.

So despite the fact that diet books often recommend flesh foods as part of a "balanced diet," and the

United States Department of Agriculture (USDA) naturally finds a place for them in its old "food pyramid" and new "food plate," the basic science here is simple: these foods are not good for you or your waistline. They provide no nutrients that you can't obtain elsewhere, in better form, without the saturated fat and cholesterol. They are obviously a contributing factor in the epidemics of obesity and heart disease. And so, as we say at the Wellness Forum, if you're going to consume any animal foods at all, they should be no more than a "condiment" in your diet. I choose to eat none at all, and you will find no animal ingredients in the recipe section.

Now hold on, Del, I hear you saying. *You ate yourself to 475 pounds without eating any flesh foods!* Yes, I did. Let's examine how I achieved it.

To do so, let's look now at how baked goods, like scones and muffins and cookies, which were central to my vegan diet while I was packing on the pounds, stack up against our dietary objectives. Traditionally, they almost always have excessive fat, usually from oil or shortening and sometimes from chocolate and nuts or seeds as well. Some of that fat is saturated. By definition, these are products that are excessive in flour, so they are highly caloric. By definition, these are processed foods, prepared by mixing together such processed ingredients as oils and flour. They are always made with concentrated sugars of one form or another. And they tend to be deficient in fiber and phytochemicals.

So, without eating any flesh foods, I ate myself into morbid obesity by breaking the following rules: excessive fats (oils, margarine, coconut, chocolate, avocado, and nuts), excessive flours, overly processed foods, and way, way too much sugar. So while my brother made it to the 400-pound range with the excessive fat in animal foods, I did it without the animal foods. There are many different paths to obesity, different rules to violate, but they bring you to the same unhappy end.

Let's compare an example of the kind of food people eat on the Standard American Diet, with a "healthy treat" that can be found in health food stores. Let's compare Burger King's Triple Whopper Sandwich with Cheese to a raw organic vegan chocolate mousse that I came across in a health food store. The Triple Whopper has 1,230 calories, 740 of which (or 60 percent) come from fat. To put that in perspective, a healthy 2,000-calorie-per-day diet would contain about 300 calories from fat, so this one sandwich provides about two and a half days' worth of fat. But not just any old fat: it's got killer fat. It's loaded with 32 grams of saturated fat. As there's no need for saturated fat in the human diet, this is truly the stuff of heart attacks. As a rule, I eat no saturated fat at all, but most people could probably get away with eating, say, 1 or 2 grams of saturated fat per day without consequence. By that standard, the Triple Whopper provides about a month's worth of saturated fat in one sandwich. It also contains 205 mg of cholesterol and 1,550 mg of sodium. It offers a lowly 3 grams of fiber. It's not really a sandwich at all; it's more nearly a weapon. It's almost unbelievable that a sandwich so off-the-scale unhealthy can be offered as food by a restaurant. Start with 740 calories from fat, including 32 grams of saturated fat, and then add fries to that, and wash it down with a milkshake! It's mind-boggling.

Now let's move on to the healthy-sounding raw organic vegan chocolate mousse that I found in a local health food store. Raw is good, and organic is terrific, right? And the treat is made from simple ingredients: coconut milk, coconut oil, dates, and cacao. No artificial chemicals, preservatives, or stabilizers. How could you go wrong with a wholesome treat like this?

Well, a 2-ounce serving provides 288 calories, 216 of which (or 75 percent) come from fat. There are 21 grams of saturated fat and 1 gram of fiber.

Triple Whopper	Vegan Chocolate Mousse (2 oz.)
1,230 calories	288 calories
740 calories from fat (60 percent)	216 calories from fat (75 percent)
32 g saturated fat	21 g saturated fat
205 mg cholesterol	0 mg cholesterol
1,550 mg sodium	5,000 mg sodium
3 g fiber	1 g fiber

But I'll bet almost no one eats just one serving since a small plastic container allegedly contains two servings. And remember, the stuff is undoubtedly scrumptious, especially for those accustomed to sweets and fatty foods. So for the average consumer who eats the entire contents of the container, double the numbers on the chart. Now we're up to 42 grams of saturated fat. That's more saturated fat than found in the Burger King Triple Whopper Sandwich with Cheese. In fact, in terms of saturated fat, a small container of the vegan mousse would be roughly equivalent to a *Quadruple* Whopper. Frightening stuff.

You will hear proponents of raw food laud the benefits of such products as coconut oil. Don't believe it.

Dietary Food Choices

It should be clear by now that we need to avoid or minimize flesh foods, oils, and sugars. We also need to keep a watchful eye on processed foods and foods made from flour. But what should we eat in their place? What should the daily fare be?

The optimal diet is a low-fat, plant-based diet. Fruits, vegetables, legumes (lentils, peas, and beans), and whole grains are the food groups on which we need to base our diet. But we need to do so by making sure that we are satisfying ourselves, not leaving ourselves hungry. Starchy vegetables like corn, potatoes, and sweet potatoes are excellent for satisfying hunger.

Beans also are very filling. Whole-grain foods also will satisfy the appetite, whether it's brown rice, buckwheat, barley, corn, or any other whole grain. These are the foods that you want to eat plenty of. Without a sufficient intake of these appetite-satisfying foods, you are likely to fail on a plant-based diet because it's hard, if not impossible, to be satisfied with just fruit and non-starchy vegetables. Leafy green salads and fruit are wonderfully healthy foods, but if you try to live on them exclusively, you'll likely drive yourself nuts with hunger in short order.

If you need to lose weight, here's a simple way of understanding why foods like beans and potatoes will drive your weight loss. It takes about 3,400 calories to fill up on meat and cheese at any given time, whereas it takes about 400 to 500 calories of high-fiber foods like beans and potatoes to fill the stomach. That's why at the Wellness Forum, we put these starchy whole foods at the base of our Food Pyramid and emphasize their centrality to the diet.

I try to eat on a regular basis whether I get hungry or not. I think in terms of having several small meals daily so that the negative connotation of "snacking" doesn't

The Restaurant Dilemma

Don't outsource your health to restaurants. Keep in mind, especially if you are trying to lose weight or to improve your health, that American restaurants are not primarily in the business of keeping you compliant on a diet that is, in so many ways, the opposite of standard American fare. They are not in the business of restoring you to health. There may be exceptions here and there—the occasional restaurant that you can trust—but it's rare to find restaurants that will prepare meals for you without oil. Even if they try, is anyone in the kitchen looking to see if there's oil in the sauce? (I can almost promise you that there's going to be oil in the sauce.) I have to admit that when my own weight loss progress has been stalled, it's often been because I've allowed myself to order takeout or to dine in restaurants too often. Restaurants can be particularly treacherous for individuals first transitioning to a new way of eating. At that stage, you need to be even more vigilant to avoid lapsing into noncompliance

come into play, and hunger doesn't let me go astray and rule my food choices. I know that the worst mistake I can make is to let myself grow ravenous, when I might make poor food choices.

Keeping Hunger Away

While it may be necessary or desirable to go to restaurants now and then, you should mostly be shopping for

and failing to achieve results. You need to have complete or nearly complete control over the foods that you are ingesting.

Of course, it's hard to avoid restaurants entirely, and you may not want to or be able to; after all, it's a convenient way to meet with friends, and business lunches are unavoidable for many people. So choose wisely from the menu, explain clearly and very specifically your dietary preferences to the waiter to get a feel for what's possible, and, very importantly, ask for all your dressings and sauces on the side, and keep them on the side. Restaurants can really screw up a good meal by pouring on excessive amounts of fatty dressings and sauces. Don't be a hapless victim to whatever the restaurant habitually feeds its customers; be proactive. Patronize vegan restaurants if you can, as well as restaurants that make a good-faith attempt at providing vegan options. It helps to call ahead and ask if you can be accommodated with a meal prepared without oil.

your food and thereby taking responsibility for all that will pass your lips. When you're in the grocery store, make sure that you spend more money in the produce aisle and the bulk grain section than anywhere else in the store. If your shopping cart is full of boxes and cans and jars and bottles, you're buying too much of the wrong stuff. It should be full of fruits and vegetables and whole grains and legumes.

If you have access to a farmers' market and can buy fresh, organic produce directly from growers, so much the better. If you can grow some of your own food, better still.

Here's a good money-saving tip: don't buy drinks. Give up the soda pop, fruit juice, high-energy drinks, coffee, and alcohol. Hydrate yourself only with water. You might consider investing some of the money saved on drinks in "buying up" to organic produce.

Let's say that, one evening, you don't have the time or energy for cooking, not beyond heating something up in the toaster oven. For convenience, you decide to buy some processed or prepared food—for example, a frozen veggie burger. What should you look for in the ingredient list? First, make sure it's not too long and full of words you don't recognize and can't pronounce. Second, look for whole-food ingredients: is it made from, say, brown rice and mushrooms and other whole grains and vegetables, or is it made from isolated soy protein and oils and stabilizers and sweeteners? Even prepared foods should have a healthful content of whole-food ingredients.

Watch out for the divide-and-conquer strategy employed by many manufacturers. Consumers generally know that ingredients are listed in order of weight, with the largest amount listed first. And consumers are often on the lookout for too much sugar. If the manufacturers of some prepared foods sweetened their products only with sugar, it would be at or near the top of the list of ingredients. So they divide up the sweetening agents into, for example, sugar, high-fructose corn syrup, and agave nectar. Three sweetening agents instead of one, and all of them lower on the list of ingredients than a single sweetener would be. So you have to look down the list at all the ingredients, not just the most prominent.

Next, look at the nutrition label, which can be confusing—maybe intentionally so. The nutrition label, of course, gives the calorie count per serving. While there's no need to count calories on a healthy vegan diet, a high calorie count per serving is usually indicative of a meal that's too fatty. Also, look at how many servings there are in a package. Ask yourself honestly if the number of servings in the package is realistic, or if you're more likely to eat two or three—or four—servings at a sitting. Then do the math. Now look at perhaps the most important part of the nutrition label: the number of grams of fat and saturated fat in a serving, and the calories from fat as a percentage of total calories. Ideally, you want to look for zero grams of saturated fat, but if you let yourself eat a meal (perhaps made with nuts or seeds) that has a gram or two of

saturated fat, resolve to have that be the only saturated fat you ingest all day. Make sure, too, that most of the foods you eat have either no fat, or 1 to 3 grams per serving—we want low numbers here. The key is the ratio between fat and calories. If a serving has 100 calories, ideally it will have only 10 or 15 calories from fat. That way you're keeping your percentage of calories from fat in the diet in the 10 to 15 percent range, where you want it to be. If a 100-calorie serving has 20 or 30 calories from fat, you could still eat it, especially if it's "healthy fat" from nuts or seeds, and especially if you're not trying to lose weight, but then make sure that's the fattiest food you eat all day. If it's above 30 percent of calories from fat, then watch out, especially if you're trying to lose weight.

Now here's where the nutrition labels can mislead you. For some reason, perhaps because the meat and dairy industries have undue influence over the Food and Drug Administration (FDA), which regulates the labeling of food, there is a column dedicated to the percent of Daily Value. And you will find that a food with 2 grams of saturated fat has only 10 percent of the Daily Value of saturated fat.

What's that about? Does that mean that 2 grams of saturated fat per day isn't enough, and that you should strive for 20 grams of saturated fat to meet your Daily Value?

No. This is all obfuscation and madness. A Daily Value is a recommendation by clueless bureaucrats (influenced by animal agriculture interests) of how much of a specific nutrient a person should consume in a day. The problem is that some "nutrients," like fiber, are healthful, and within reason, you really can't consume too much of them. Other "nutrients," like saturated fat, are detrimental to your health. To assign a Daily Value to saturated fat is to effectively give the seal of approval to something you should be trying to avoid. A serving of frozen crab cakes that I came across in Whole Foods apparently contains 85 mg of cholesterol, and that's considered 28 percent of the Daily Value. By my math, that would indicate that you should strive for 303 mg of cholesterol daily. But of course you shouldn't, as any sane doctor will tell you.

A small, low-fat bran muffin, also found at Whole Foods, has 13 grams of fiber, with a Daily Value of 51 percent. Does that mean that if you eat two of those muffins, you'd better not consume any more fiber all day long? Not a piece of fruit or a vegetable? That would seem to follow logically, but it's of course nonsense from a nutritional standpoint.

The Daily Value, in other words, appears to give an upper limit to nutrients that you should feel free to consume in abundance, while appearing to give a lower limit to "nutrients," like cholesterol and saturated fat, that should optimally not be present in the diet at all, or should at the very least be consumed well below that lower limit. If you consume the Daily Value for fat, for example, you'll be on a diet that has about 30 percent of its calories from fat. That's called the Standard American Diet, and it's responsible for the epidemic

of obesity plaguing the country. So instead of steering consumers toward an optimal diet, the Daily Value
serves as a confusing and misleading way of endors-
ing the very diet that has created an enormously overweight, diseased population. It's not guiding you toward
the kinds of food you should be eating; it's steering you

toward the diet of all the overweight people around you in the store.

So don't look at the Daily Value. It's nonsense. Concentrate on the ingredients themselves, the amount of fat and saturated fat, and the percentage of calories from fat.

Of course, the less processed food you purchase, the less you have to worry about misleading nutrition labels. There are no nutrition labels on fresh produce. That's where you should be doing the bulk of your shopping—the produce aisles and the grain aisles. Clear your kitchen as much as possible of all the processed products and make way for some real food.

Cooking
with Plants

Now let's go over in detail most of the kitchen tools, ingredients, and techniques I use daily to cook with plant foods and maintain a diet that is, indeed, better than vegan.

Cookware and Knives

Nothing exotic or expensive in the way of cookware is required for the recipes in this book or for creating healthy, plant-based cuisine generally. You'll need an inexpensive collection of pots and pans, stockpots in two or three sizes (a 6-quart, 4-quart, and maybe 3-quart pot), sauté skillets or saucepans in a couple of sizes, baking sheets, baking pans, and casserole pans. You'll also need a food processor and a blender.

While there's no need to buy the most expensive kitchenware, do try to avoid aluminum. I use stainless steel, cast-iron, or enamel-coated pans. You might want to own a good-quality nonstick pan made from ceramic nonstick materials.

I recommend the use of three knives: one, a chef's knife—a large knife for chopping, dicing, and mincing; two, a paring knife, for peeling vegetables or fruit, or for cutting the eyes out of a potato; and three, a serrated knife, for slicing fresh bread or lasagna.

Pantry

A healthy pantry will contain some basic foods: To begin with, a collection of grains (rice, millet, barley, wheat berries, quinoa, buckwheat groats, spelt berries, rolled oats). Next, a collection of dried beans and canned beans (if budget is an issue, dried beans are cheaper than canned; if time is an issue, canned beans can save you a lot of it) and a supply of peas and lentils. Tomatoes are fundamental, and remember that cooked tomatoes provide you with more cancer-fighting lycopene than raw; you'll want to have canned diced tomatoes, tomato purée, and tomato paste on hand. You should be continually refreshing your supply of some inexpensive basics from the produce aisles: potatoes, sweet potatoes, yams, onions, carrots, celery, and garlic. I also like to keep a good supply of low-sodium soup stock, balsamic vinegar, and brown rice vinegar available.

You'll also want to have a collection of plant milks. Discover which ones work best for you. There are plenty of varieties: rice, soy, hemp, almond, and oat milks. I personally try to avoid the fortified varieties, since the health "benefits" of fortification are unclear at best. Try to buy plant milks that are unsweetened, or only lightly sweetened, and made without oil. Look for the grams of sugar as well as the grams of fat per serving, and aim for low numbers.

To make the dishes flavorful, we need a collection of spices: dried allspice, dried basil, cinnamon, cloves, granulated garlic, dried ginger, turmeric, dried mustard power, tarragon, thyme, oregano, fenugreek, nutmeg, cardamom, bay leaves, marjoram, crushed red pepper, cayenne pepper, black pepper, ancho chili powder, chipotle chili powder or dried chipotles, coriander seeds, onion powder, paprika, smoked paprika, sweet paprika, smoked jalapeño, rosemary, sage, and saffron, the world's most expensive spice.

For sweeteners, we'll use dates, maple syrup, very ripe bananas, and stevia. Unsweetened cocoa powder comes in handy for desserts, as does silken tofu, which comes in a box and does not have to be refrigerated. I use lite silken tofu, which is lower in fat. For salty seasoning, get some good, naturally brewed tamari, Bragg's Liquid Aminos, and your favorite sea salt.

Whole-grain flours made from wheat (including whole-wheat pastry flour), spelt, or brown rice will be needed on occasion.

Refrigerated and Frozen Items

In the refrigerator, we need to always have a supply of fresh vegetables. Condiments like ketchup, mustard, sweet pickle relish, and salsa are nice to have on hand. Miso paste is a refrigerated item used in a lot of dishes. Mellow white miso is my personal favorite. I also usually have a supply of homemade soup stock in my refrigerator. All forms of tofu except silken tofu require refrigeration, as does tempeh. Make sure your refrigerator is below 40 degrees F.

In the freezer, you'll want to keep an array of frozen vegetables: corn, green peas, asparagus, broccoli, and chopped spinach, for example. I don't worry over whether a vegetable is frozen or fresh. Science tells us that it's much more important to eat vegetables than to differentiate between frozen and fresh. And remember: our goal is to make eating a whole-foods diet as easy as possible. That's why I also rely on having frozen fruits in the freezer for smoothies. Corn tortillas, or whole-wheat or spelt flour tortillas, can generally be found in my freezer as well, and come in handy not only for Mexican dishes but anytime you're looking for a bread substitute.

Science tells us that it's much more important to eat vegetables than to differentiate between frozen and fresh.

Kitchen Principles

Keep your kitchen and your utensils clean. Scrub fruits and vegetables well. Stock and organize your kitchen in accordance with the key principle that you want to eat more often with smaller portions. The longer you go between eating, the more calories you're likely to ultimately consume. Eating smaller meals throughout the day helps maintain a healthy glucose level and keeps hunger at bay. That means keeping healthy quick-bite items (fat-free hummus, cucumbers, baby carrots, fat-free rice crackers, rice cakes, fruit) around at all times (and taking what you need with you to work).

Kitchen "No-Nos"

Here's a partial list of some of the things you won't find in my kitchen: cooking oils, margarine, sugar, white flour, animal products, coconut, avocado, or processed foods made with any of the aforementioned ingredients. Also not to be found: a microwave oven. So you won't need any of those items for any recipe in this book.

Substitutions

Use the recipes in this book as templates; feel free to make substitutions. Once you understand the concepts behind the style of cooking, it will be easy to do. Tempeh and tofu (but not silken tofu) and seitan can be interchanged in many dishes, though they need to be treated a little differently. Potatoes can be swapped for sweet potatoes or yams. Switch one type of bean for another or one type of grain for another. If you don't like cumin, try coriander. My Jicama Slaw (page 256) can be made with cabbage, carrots, or beets. My Creamy Pasta and Broccoli (page 226) can be made with zucchini. Feel free to substitute baked tofu for seitan in my Tropical "Chicken" Salad (page 201).

Some recipes may remind you of the sorts of dishes one might encounter in a standard American cookbook, but with substitutions made to keep the dishes healthy. Instead of making cream sauces with dairy, we can use silken tofu, purée it, and thin it out with soymilk. Or we can take almond milk and add a little arrowroot to it, and it thickens into a cream sauce. To make soups creamier, we can add potato flakes or puréed cauliflower. To add a cheesy flavor, nutritional yeast can help. (Cashew creams are very popular now in vegan cuisine, but the fat is excessive. Silken tofu, by contrast, is lower in fat than traditional tofu, and Nasoya makes a lite tofu with reduced fat.) Beans can be puréed into a gravy, making a nice alternative to fatty gravies, high in fiber and full of flavor. Kombu can be added to bean dishes as a tenderizer. To replace eggs in baking, we can use apple-

sauce or commercial egg replacer. Flaxseeds can also serve as an egg replacer after being blended up with water. Milk can be replaced by any kind of plant milk.

While you should feel free to be creative, how you stray from the recipes can be important. Until you've really mastered all the techniques involved in this style of cooking, you might not want to substitute more than one or two ingredients in any dish. Ultimately, it's the technique that's more important than any given recipe. Once you get the technique and the principles of low-fat cooking down, you can give yourself freer range to experiment.

Cooking Techniques

What differentiates this cookbook from most vegetarian or vegan cookbooks, more than anything else, is the absence of oil in the recipes. The only challenging aspect of oil-free cooking is in sautéing, because that's where most of us were taught to rely on olive or canola oil or other "cooking" oils.

Sautéing without oil is a pretty straightforward process, whether you're sautéing vegetables as a side dish or doing a stir-fry. You start out with a dry pan and make it warm. Keep in mind that some vegetables have more water in them than others. Onions, carrots, peppers, mushrooms, fennel, beets, and celery have high water contents, so they tend to do quite well in that

oil-free environment. Add vegetables in order of their cooking time, and try to factor in how much water is in the vegetables. Higher-water-content vegetables go in the pan first, and the low-water-content vegetables generally go last—eggplant, broccoli, snow peas, potatoes, sweet potatoes, cauliflower, zucchini. It's a good idea, for example, to put onions and carrots in first, since they are water rich and have a long cooking time. Use the water-rich vegetables to help provide liquid for the cooking of water-deficient vegetables. Sauté broccoli with onion, for example, and sauté cauliflower with

mushrooms. You should need to add very little liquid to the pan when you sauté. A residue will build up on the bottom of the pan—that's caramelization—and you should scrape the brown off the bottom of the pan as you cook and retain those flavors in the dish.

Another technique is to steam or parboil slow-cooking vegetables such as broccoli or cauliflower first before putting them in the sauté pan.

If you're doing a stir-fry instead of sautéing, it's a hotter and quicker process. Get the pan or wok very hot before putting the vegetables in, and then stir them around quickly when you do. Add water as needed, while trying to allow some caramelization to take place. For me, stir-fries change by the season according to what's available fresh. I tend to cook according to what's available in my garden. When I have fresh basil or tomatoes in my garden, I toss them in my stir-fry. If there's a good variety of fresh mushrooms at the farmers' market at a low price, they're destined for my wok. But if not, you can still make a healthy stir-fry even with a package of frozen vegetables. Learning how to make an oil-free stir-fry is a great foundation for many of the recipes you'll find in this book.

Braising vegetables can add flavor to food, especially when you do so with a vegetable stock or wine with fresh or dried herbs. Braising is recommended for longer cooking times in dishes that don't "fry" well. Potatoes or root vegetables in a stew do well with braising.

Baking or roasting accomplishes many of the same effects as sautéing. It browns the dish, removes water, and concentrates flavor. Casseroles like lasagna do well with baking. While roasting vegetables is a popular way to cook them, doing so without oil can be a little tricky because of the drying effect of the technique. Using a combination of braising and roasting is a good way to cook vegetables when you want a roasted flavor; the braising cooks the vegetables and then you can finish them and caramelize them by roasting (although not long enough to dry them out).

Stewing is the technique of slow-cooking ingredients in a broth. Vegetables such as those in a *mirepoix* are popular in many stews as well as soups because they make a great foundation upon which to build flavor. As herbs and spices are added to the broth, the flavors all marry to create a dish with all the nuances of taste that you desire.

Soup's On

Soups can be meals in themselves and have the benefit of satisfying the appetite and hydrating you at the same time. Soups can truly help you lose weight, but that doesn't mean that you have to confine yourself to all-you-can-eat cabbage soup; almost any soup can serve the purpose. Often I begin with a *mirepoix,* the classic foundation in French cooking of onions, carrots, and celery, which I sauté and brown before adding to a soup stock. From there we can go in any number of directions: a bean, vegetable, lentil, or potato soup, for example. Often I'll begin making a soup without knowing in which direction I'm going to turn.

Selecting Your Ingredients

Along with cooking techniques, choosing the right ingredients can go a long way in creating a successful dish. Fresh vegetables bought in season taste better than those out of season. Leeks are one of my favorite sauce starters because they have an amazing flavor that does not need much help. And fresh or dried herbs, along with spices, are important aspects of most of my recipes because they add flavor without adding fat or salt. Think of herbs and spices as the healthy way to add flavor: many are high in antioxidants. Condiments such as mustard (regular or Dijon), vinegars, pickle relishes, and capers, are some of the many flavor builders for my dishes, whether they are used within the recipe itself or as a garnish. And don't forget that, as we down-regulate our taste buds, the natural flavor in food comes out, so we find that fresh fruit is sweet enough, and we reduce or eliminate our desire for sugar and processed foods.

Timing

Timing is one of the keys to successful cooking, and with greater experience and mastery of the art, many of the concepts involved in the timing of cooking become second nature and your own time can be used more efficiently in the kitchen. If you are just starting out, I would recommend that you have all ingredients prepared—washed, cut if necessary, measured, and set out before you—before you begin firing up the burners.

Seasoning

There are plenty of profoundly unhealthy ways to add flavor to meals. It's too often accomplished by adding fat, milk, or meat to a dish. Frying is popular because it's an easy way to get flavor out of food. Adding butter or oil to baked goods makes them tender and gives them a good mouthfeel. Sugar not only tastes good but is addictive and leaves us feeling hungry for more. So our challenge is: how do we make food taste good without ruining our health?

Seasoning is the answer.

Seasoning happens at every level of cooking, and different cooking techniques yield different results in terms of adding flavors. I start many of my recipes by sautéing vegetables because sautéing or stir-frying without oil caramelizes the food being cooked, removes water from it, and therefore concentrates flavor. That is why a stir-fry doesn't need a heavy sauce to make it taste good; all the same, stir-fry dishes in America tend to be heavy with sauces, and unnecessarily so.

Spices generally are seeds or roots, and can be added early on because their flavors are hardy enough to withstand the cooking process. Herbs are leaves of plants, and many, such as oregano, sage, thyme, and marjoram, also hold up well to the cooking process. Others,

such as basil and cilantro, are tender. If you want basil to stand atop the flavor profile, add it at the end; add it earlier if you want it to be embedded in the dish to marry with the other flavors.

In Thai cooking, for example, you don't want any single flavor to stand out. Garlic and onions should be added early on. Onions become sweeter as they caramelize; garlic becomes more mellow. Letting the garlic brown is an option that some prefer.

Toasting spices produces a pungent flavor that many like. You can dry-toast cumin seeds and oregano by putting them in a dry skillet on the stove at medium heat. When you start to smell them, they're done.

In dishes where you want the flavor of garlic and onions to be stronger, adding fresh chopped garlic or onion at the end is the appropriate way to go.

Dried herbs and spices are more powerful than fresh. Flavors are concentrated when dried. Use about one-third as much of dried seasonings as you would use of fresh. Dried are more expensive than fresh, but more readily available. Dried herbs do not last forever, however; after about a year, their oils lose their volatility. Therefore, where you buy your dried herbs is important; they can go stale on the shelf. I buy mine at a food co-op where I know they have a high turnover. If you buy dried basil, for example, and it doesn't smell like basil, it's probably too old.

Cilantro does not hold up well in dried form; always use it fresh. When fresh herbs and spices are available, I prefer to go that route.

Ginger is among the more powerful of spices, so be careful not to overdo its use.

I recommend the use of a microplane to grate ginger. I never buy ginger in a jar; I buy it fresh. If you're buying young ginger, you don't have to peel the skin before you use it. Younger ginger has thinner skin.

Freshly ground black pepper is a completely different animal, to use a non-vegan expression, than pre-ground black pepper. I prefer to use freshly ground.

Most spices are best freshly ground: coriander, cumin, black pepper, cardamom, nutmeg, and mace. I believe that when you choose fresh, you're better off from both taste and health standpoints.

Although I don't practice salt restriction, I advise adding salt toward the end of cooking, so that you'll use less. If you add salt, for example, to boiling water when boiling vegetables, as the water evaporates you'll wind up with higher and higher salt concentration; that's why it's better to add it toward the end when you can salt to taste in more moderate amounts. Rather than iodized salt or table salt, which may contain aluminum silicates, I recommend sea salt.

And now it's time to get cooking.

Recipes

The fun begins.

Sauces, Dips, Creams, and Dressings

We're putting these first, since they will garnish and
complete many dishes that follow.

Cauliflower Purée

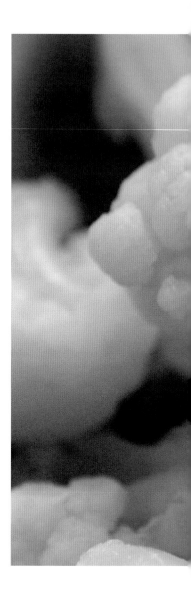

Traditional white sauces are made from cream or milk. Vegan white sauces are usually made with plant milk or silken tofu. My favorite white sauce is made from cauliflower purée. It is one of the most adaptable sauces I make, and much like its dairy-based counterpart, it takes on the flavor of whatever you use to season it.

3 cups cauliflower florets
¾ to 1 cup water, vegetable stock, or Basic Soup
    Stock (page 146)
Sea salt to taste

Place the cauliflower in a steamer and cook until very tender, about 8 to 10 minutes. Place the florets in a blender and purée with enough water to make a creamy consistency. Season with salt.

VARIATION

Coconut-Cauliflower Purée

Add ½ teaspoon coconut extract to the blender and purée with the cauliflower and water.

Black Bean Burrito (page 180) and
Chipotle Cream Sauce (page 76)

Chipotle Cream Sauce

See photo on pages 74–75.

I love the smoky, spicy flavor this sauce adds to Mushroom Tacos with Chipotle Cream (page 208). But I also eat it on baked potatoes or sautéed vegetables—just for kicks!

2 chipotle peppers in adobo sauce
1 cup Cauliflower Purée (page 72)
3 shallots, minced
2 cloves garlic, minced
¼ cup dry white wine
Sea salt and black pepper to taste

Pureé the chipotle peppers in adobo sauce with the cauliflower purée until smooth and creamy. Set aside. Sauté the shallots over medium heat in a medium skillet until tender, about 5 minutes. Add water 1 to 2 tablespoons at a time to keep the shallots from sticking. Add the garlic and cook for another minute. Add the wine and cook until it is almost evaporated. Add the cauliflower purée and chipotle peppers, and cook over medium-low heat for 5 minutes. Season with salt and pepper.

Hollandaise Sauce

MAKES 1¾ CUPS

See photo on page 123.

Hollandaise sauce is traditionally made with eggs and butter. This vegan version is delicious served over steamed vegetables or in my Mr. Benedict recipe (page 122).

> 1 12-ounce package extra-firm silken tofu or
>   1½ cups Cauliflower Purée (page 72)
> Zest and juice of 1 lemon
> 3 tablespoons nutritional yeast
> 1½ teaspoons sea salt
> ¼ teaspoon cayenne pepper
> ½ teaspoon turmeric

Combine all ingredients in a food processor or blender and purée until smooth and creamy. Add water if needed to make a pourable sauce. Heat the sauce in a double boiler (see note) for 10 to 12 minutes, until heated through.

Chef's Note • If you don't have a double boiler, you can put the sauce in a bowl that you then place over a saucepan of gently boiling water. Make sure the bowl only partially fits in the saucepan so that the bottom of the bowl does not touch the boiling water.

Creamy Leek Sauce

MAKES 2½ CUPS

Toss this flavorful sauce with cooked pasta or sautéed vegetables, or serve it as a topping for baked potatoes.

2 large leeks, thinly sliced
½ teaspoon thyme, minced
Pinch of ground nutmeg
2 cups Cauliflower Purée (page 72)
Sea salt and black pepper to taste

In a large saucepan, sauté the leeks over medium heat for 7 to 8 minutes. Add water 1 to 2 tablespoons at a time to keep the leeks from sticking. Add the thyme and nutmeg and cook for 1 minute. Add the cauliflower purée and cook over medium-low heat for 5 minutes. Season with salt and pepper.

Garden Fresh Tomato Sauce

I make this sauce in the summer when I have more tomatoes in the garden than I can eat on salads. I eat it on pasta or use it as a sauce for lasagna.

1 large onion, diced

2 medium carrots, peeled and diced

2 stalks celery, diced

6 cloves garlic, minced

12 large ripe tomatoes, chopped

2 tablespoons tomato paste

1½ cups chopped fresh basil

2 teaspoons thyme, minced

2 teaspoons oregano, minced

1 bay leaf

Sea salt and black pepper to taste

Sauté the onion, carrots, and celery over medium heat for 10 to 12 minutes. Add water 1 to 2 tablespoons at a time to keep the vegetables from sticking. Add the garlic and cook for 2 minutes. Add the remaining ingredients and bring to a boil. Decrease the heat to low and cook the sauce, partially covered, for 1 hour.

The Best Date Syrup Ever

MAKES 3 CUPS

Dates are nature's candy and a great natural sweetener. Medjool dates are sweeter than other dates, and stevia gives this recipe extra sweetening power, so I can use less of this calorie-dense treat. Use this date syrup as a sweetener in place of your regular sugar, or add a little vanilla extract to it and use it as a topping for ice cream (pages 266–267).

2 cups pitted Medjool dates
½ teaspoon stevia powder
1½ to 2 cups water

Place all ingredients in a blender and purée until smooth and creamy. Add water as needed to get the mixture to blend. Store refrigerated for up to one week.

Low-Fat Mayonnaise

Mayonnaise is a popular condiment in American cuisine and is served on or in everything from hamburgers to potato salad. This simple sauce, made here with cauliflower purée, comes together quickly and will keep refrigerated for seven days.

2 tablespoons red wine vinegar

2 teaspoons Dijon mustard

2 cloves garlic, minced

1 teaspoon granulated onion

1 teaspoon sea salt

1½ cups Cauliflower Purée (page 72) or
    1 12-ounce package firm silken tofu

Combine all ingredients in a food processor and purée until smooth and creamy. Refrigerate.

Jalapeño Mayonnaise

See photo on page 250.

You can't make a good Black Bean Burger (page 204) without a good mayo to complement it. Well, here it is.

1 cup Low-Fat Mayonnaise (page 84)
2 jalapeño peppers, seeded and finely chopped
4 tablespoons chopped fresh cilantro
Zest of 2 limes

Combine everything in a blender and purée until smooth and creamy. Store refrigerated in an airtight container for up to seven days.

Maple Cream

See photo on page 107.

This is one of my favorite dessert sauces. It is great on my Big Fat Breakfast Pizza (page 115) and as a topping for fruit salad.

1 12-ounce package lite silken tofu

½ teaspoon ground cinnamon

½ teaspoon vanilla extract

¼ cup plus 2 tablespoons maple syrup or Best Date Syrup Ever (page 83)

Pinch of sea salt

Blend together all ingredients in a food processor until smooth and creamy. Store refrigerated in an airtight container for up to seven days.

Creamy Dijon Vinaigrette

I love this dressing on everything from steamed brussels sprouts and asparagus to potato salad or a simple mixed greens salad.

1½ cups Cauliflower Purée (page 72)
⅓ cup Dijon mustard
Zest of 1 lemon
2 large shallots, minced
1 tablespoon minced fresh tarragon
Sea salt and black pepper to taste

Combine everything in a food processor and purée until smooth and creamy. Store refrigerated in an airtight container for up to seven days.

Ginger-Miso Dressing (page 95)
Thousand Island Dressing (page 94)
Creamy Dijon Vinaigrette

Cucumber Dressing

White beans are an unusual ingredient in a salad dressing, but they make it filling, and no one will know the difference. And you don't have to tell them.

1 cup cooked white beans
¼ cup fresh lemon juice
Zest of 1 lemon
2 large cucumbers, peeled, seeded, and
   coarsely chopped
1 clove garlic
Sea salt to taste
Pinch of cayenne pepper

Combine all ingredients in a blender and purée until smooth and creamy. Store refrigerated in an airtight container for up to seven days.

Ranch Dressing

The 10 minutes it takes to make this better-than-bottled ranch dressing is worth the effort, and if you are a ranch-dressing fanatic, make a double batch to use as a dip for veggies.

1½ cups Cauliflower Purée (page 72)
¼ cup white wine vinegar
4 green onions, chopped
2 tablespoons chopped chives
1 tablespoon chopped fresh tarragon
2 cloves garlic, minced
Sea salt and black pepper to taste

Combine everything in a blender and purée until smooth and creamy. Store refrigerated in an air-tight container for up to seven days.

Thousand Island Dressing

MAKES 2 CUPS

See photo on page 89.

A popular salad dressing since the 1950s, Thousand Island is my favorite when I want a vegan Reuben.

1½ cups Cauliflower Purée (page 72)
½ teaspoon ground mustard
¼ cup red wine vinegar
¼ cup tomato purée
1 clove garlic, minced
½ teaspoon paprika
½ teaspoon prepared horseradish
½ teaspoon vegan Worcestershire sauce
½ cup Best Date Syrup Ever (page 83)

Combine all ingredients in a food processor and purée until smooth and creamy. Store refrigerated in an airtight container for up to seven days.

Ginger-Miso Dressing

See photo on page 89.

This ginger-miso dressing is great on a salad, as a dip for vegetables, or even as a sauce for stir-fries.

1 cup Cauliflower Purée (page 72)

⅔ cup brown rice vinegar

¼ cup mellow white miso

4 large cloves garlic, peeled

2 tablespoons minced fresh ginger

2 tablespoons brown rice syrup

½ teaspoon cayenne pepper

Combine all ingredients in a food processor and purée until smooth and creamy. Store refrigerated in an airtight container for up to seven days.

Mango Salad Dressing

This makes a fine dressing for a salad or a fantastic dip for fruit.

2 large mangoes, peeled, seeded, and
    coarsely chopped
½ cup fresh orange juice
½ cup rice wine vinegar
¼ cup brown rice syrup
¼ teaspoon sea salt
¼ teaspoon crushed red pepper

Combine all ingredients in a blender and purée until smooth and creamy. Store refrigerated in an airtight container for up to seven days.

The Best Mushroom Gravy Ever

SERVES 6 TO 8

This gravy is my go-to sauce during the holidays when I want a lot of flavor without all the fat. Porcini mushrooms give any dish an earthy flavor without a lot of effort—yum!!!

1 ounce dried porcini mushrooms

1 cup hot water

2 shallots, minced

8 ounces cremini mushrooms (about 3–3½ cups), sliced

4 tablespoons arrowroot powder whisked together with ¼ cup cold water

2½ cups vegetable stock or Basic Soup Stock (page 146)

6 tablespoons dry sherry

Sea salt and black pepper to taste

Place the dried porcini mushrooms in a medium bowl and pour the hot water over them. Let stand for about 30 minutes. Strain the mushrooms and reserve the liquid. Coarsely chop the mushrooms.

(continued on following page)

The Best Mushroom Gravy Ever drizzled over Del's Stuffed "Beast" (page 230)

(continued from previous page)

Sauté the shallots, porcini mushrooms, and cremini mushrooms over medium-high heat for 7 to 8 minutes. Add water 1 to 2 tablespoons at a time as needed to keep the vegetables from sticking. Add the arrowroot mixture, vegetable stock, ½ cup of the reserved porcini mushroom soaking liquid, and sherry, and bring the gravy to a boil. Cook until thickened and remove from the heat. Season with salt and pepper.

Serve hot.

Chili Gravy

This is my favorite enchilada gravy. It's not too spicy, but you can add some heat with a little cayenne pepper, and it has that rich creamy texture without the cream.

1 small yellow onion, minced

2 cloves garlic, minced

1½ tablespoons ancho chili powder

2 teaspoons ground cumin

½ teaspoon oregano

3 cups Cauliflower Purée (page 72)

Sea salt and black pepper to taste

Sauté the onion over medium heat for 10 minutes. Add water 1 to 2 tablespoons at a time to keep the onion from sticking. Add the garlic, chili powder, cumin, and oregano, and cook for another minute. Add the cauliflower purée and cook for 2 to 4 minutes until the sauce is hot. Season with salt and pepper.

Mango-Ginger Smoothie (page 104)
Cocoa-Almond Smoothie (page 105)

Breakfasts

Mango-Ginger Smoothie

SERVES 2

Smoothies are quick and easy meals any time of day, but they are perfect for breakfast because they come together so quickly.

  1½ cups unsweetened plant milk

  2 cups frozen mango chunks

  1 banana, sliced

  Best Date Syrup Ever (page 83) to taste

  1 tablespoon grated fresh ginger, or use more or
    less to taste

Add everything to a blender and process until smooth and creamy.

Cocoa-Almond Smoothie

SERVES 2

Here's a smoothie that could be a breakfast or a dessert.

1½ to 2 cups unsweetened plant milk

2 cups frozen banana slices

Best Date Syrup Ever (page 83) to taste

2 tablespoons unsweetened cocoa powder

¼ teaspoon almond extract

Add everything to a blender and process until smooth and creamy.

Banana-Maple Granola

SERVES 8

This is my favorite granola. It is easy to make and has great flavor.

2 ripe bananas
½ cup maple syrup or Best Date Syrup Ever
   (page 83)
¼ cup water
1 teaspoon vanilla extract
Pinch of sea salt
4 cups rolled oats

Preheat the oven to 300 degrees F. Line a 13 × 18 inch baking sheet with parchment paper and set aside.

Combine the bananas, maple or date syrup, water, vanilla, and salt in a food processor and purée until the mixture is smooth and creamy. Add the banana purée to a bowl with the oats and mix well. Spread the mixture onto the prepared baking sheet. Bake the granola for 40 to 45 minutes. Let cool and store in a sealed container for up to ten days.

Banana-Maple Granola and Maple Cream (page 87)

Fruit and Spice Breakfast Bars

MAKES 8 BARS

These cane-sugar-free, fruit-filled bars are great for breakfast on the go. Wrap the uneaten bars in plastic and put them in an airtight container and they will keep for two or three days.

1 cup whole-wheat pastry flour

1 cup barley flour

1 tablespoon baking powder

1 teaspoon ground cinnamon

1 teaspoon ground ginger

¼ teaspoon ground cloves

¼ teaspoon sea salt

1 cup Best Date Syrup Ever (page 83)

¾ cup applesauce

1 teaspoon orange zest

1 teaspoon almond extract

½ cup chopped Medjool dates

½ cup chopped dried apricots

½ cup raisins

(continued on following page)

(continued from previous page)

Preheat the oven to 350 degrees F. Line an
8 × 8 inch square baking pan with parchment
paper and set aside.

Put the flours, baking powder, cinnamon,
ginger, cloves, and salt in a bowl and combine
well. In another bowl, combine the date syrup,
applesauce, orange zest, and almond extract
and mix well. Gently fold the applesauce mixture
and the dates, apricots, and raisins into the flour
mixture. Spread the batter in the prepared pan
and bake for 30 to 35 minutes, until a toothpick
inserted in the center of the pan comes out clean.
Let cool before cutting into squares.

Basic Oatmeal

Oatmeal is the ultimate healthy fast-food breakfast. It is quick to prepare, filling, and inexpensive. Add your favorite fresh or dried fruit to the oatmeal while it cooks to give it some flair. I like chopped dates or figs and banana.

I used to eat oatmeal drenched in milk, butter, and sugar. The oats were probably more of a garnish for the fat and sugar topping I served it with. I still don't eat plain oatmeal, but my new toppings are a lot more healthful than my old ones—and just as tasty.

1 cup water
½ cup rolled oats
½ teaspoon ground cinnamon
Sea salt to taste

Bring the water to a boil in a small saucepan and add the oats and cinnamon. Cover the pan and bring it to a boil over medium heat. Cook for 5 minutes. Add salt to taste.

Oatmeal with Poached Rhubarb

SERVES 6

I make this dish only on weekends in the spring when rhubarb is in season. I make a big batch of the poached rhubarb and use the extra as a dessert sauce for my Very Berry Ice Cream recipe (page 266).

1½ pounds rhubarb, peeled if necessary, and cut into 3- or 4-inch stalks

¼ cup water

1½ cups Best Date Syrup Ever (page 83), or more to taste

Dash of sea salt

6 servings cooked oatmeal (page 111)

Combine the rhubarb and water in a medium saucepan and bring to a boil over medium heat. Let the mixture simmer for 5 minutes, then add the date syrup and salt. Cook, covered, for 8 to 10 minutes, until the rhubarb is tender. Purée in a blender with a tight-fitting lid, covered with a towel over the lid (to keep the hot liquid from splattering). Spoon over prepared oatmeal or your favorite ice cream.

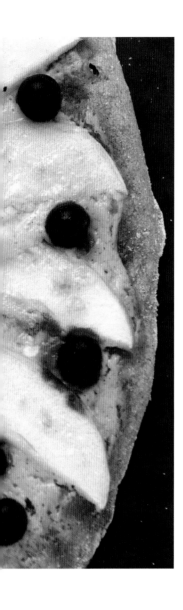

Big Fat Breakfast Pizza

SERVES 4

Pizza is not a typical breakfast, but, hey, this is not your typical pizza.

1 10-ounce jar sugar-free apricot fruit spread

1 cup Maple Cream (page 87)

1 prebaked 12-inch crust made with Whole-Wheat Pizza Dough (page 186)

1 pint fresh strawberries, sliced

2 kiwis, peeled and sliced

1 Granny Smith apple, thinly sliced

½ pint blueberries

Preheat the oven to 375 degrees F.

Heat the fruit spread in a small saucepan until it is liquefied. Spread the maple cream over the crust and arrange the fresh fruits decoratively on top. Brush the apricot spread over the fruits and bake the pizza for 15 to 20 minutes. Serve immediately. Do not share with anyone who criticizes you for making pizza for breakfast.

Breakfast Burritos

SERVES 4

This tofu scramble is made with lite firm tofu and then baked instead of fried, so the fat content is greatly reduced.

2 large leeks, white and light green parts only, diced into ½-inch cubes

1 medium red bell pepper, diced into ½-inch cubes

1½ cups shiitake mushrooms, stemmed and sliced

3 cloves garlic, minced

2 teaspoons ground cumin

2 teaspoons ground coriander

Black pepper to taste

2 teaspoons turmeric

2 tablespoons low-sodium soy sauce

3 tablespoons nutritional yeast

1 pound lite firm tofu, pressed and mashed to the consistency of ricotta cheese

½ cup chopped cilantro

4 10- or 12-inch whole-wheat tortillas

1 cup salsa (store-bought or your favorite homemade)

Preheat the oven to 350 degrees F.

Sauté the leeks, red bell pepper, and mushrooms over medium-high heat for 8 to 10 minutes, until the leeks are translucent and tender. Add the garlic, cumin, coriander, pepper, turmeric, soy sauce, and nutritional yeast, and cook over medium-low heat for 5 minutes. Add the tofu and mix well. Spread the mixture on a large parchment-lined baking sheet and bake for 25 to 30 minutes. Remove the scramble from the oven and stir in the cilantro.

To make the burritos, divide the scramble between the four tortillas and spoon some salsa over the filling. Fold the ends of each tortilla over the filling and roll it up.

Del's Big Breakfast Casserole

SERVES 6 TO 8

See photo on pages 120–121.

This recipe is not your everyday breakfast food. Make it for company or when you're in the mood to spend a little extra time in the kitchen on a Saturday morning.

4 medium red-skin potatoes, scrubbed and thinly sliced

3 large yellow onions, thinly sliced

1 pound firm tofu

1 12-ounce package extra-firm silken tofu

2 medium yellow onions, diced

1 red bell pepper, diced

1 8-ounce package sliced button mushrooms

1 10-ounce package frozen broccoli, thawed

4 cloves garlic, minced

1 tablespoon dried basil

1 teaspoon dried sage

½ teaspoon ground fennel seeds

1 teaspoon crushed red pepper

6 tablespoons nutritional yeast

Sea salt to taste

½ teaspoon black pepper

Preheat the oven to 350 degrees F.

Steam the potatoes for 6 to 8 minutes, until tender but still firm. While the potatoes steam, sauté the three large onions in a medium skillet until caramelized, about 12 minutes. Add water 1 to 2 tablespoons at a time to keep them from sticking. Set them aside. Place the firm tofu and silken tofu in a large bowl and mash to the consistency of ricotta cheese. Set it aside.

Heat a large skillet over medium-high heat, add the diced medium onions, red bell peppers, mushrooms, and broccoli, and sauté for 5 to 6 minutes, until the vegetables are tender. Add the garlic, basil, sage, fennel, and crushed red pepper, and cook for another minute. Add the onion mixture to the tofu along with the nutritional yeast, salt, and pepper. Mix well.

Press the tofu filling into a 9 × 13 inch nonstick baking dish. Top with the steamed potatoes and then the caramelized onions. Bake for 45 minutes.

Del's Big Breakfast Casserole (page 118)

Mr. Benedict

Mr. Benedict, as the dish is respectfully called, is a combination of spinach "ricotta" and spicy seitan. When I worked at King Avenue Coffeehouse, we had the most amazing brunch menu. One of my favorite items was our eggs Florentine, a toasted English muffin topped with a spinach-ricotta mixture, a poached egg, and a homemade hollandaise sauce. It was full of fat and dairy and was, although very tasty, very unhealthy. In this version, my tofu-spinach ricotta replaces the traditional spinach filling, a spicy seitan cutlet replaces the egg, and my version of vegan hollandaise tastes just as good as the original. I used to make a seitan sausage from scratch, but—although it's not the most time-consuming recipe—I love the ease of using premade seitan, which can still be seasoned the way I want it. Though not fat-free, this recipe is dairy-free, oil-free, and just as tasty as any you'll make with all the fatty stuff.

1 recipe Spinach "Ricotta" (recipe follows)

3 English muffins, toasted and split in half

1 recipe Spicy Seitan (recipe follows)

1¾ cups Hollandaise Sauce (page 77)

Paprika (garnish)

Chopped parsley (garnish)

To assemble the Mr. Benedict:

Preheat the oven to 350 degrees F.

Place about ½ cup spinach ricotta on each English muffin half and place each piece on a baking sheet. Cover and bake for 15 minutes, until the ricotta is heated through. Remove from the oven and place one half-muffin on each of six plates. Divide the seitan between the six muffin halves and top with the hollandaise. Sprinkle with paprika and chopped parsley for garnish.

Spinach "Ricotta"

¾ cup firm silken tofu (about ½ of a 12-ounce
package)

1 pound lite firm tofu

1 medium yellow onion, finely diced

4 cloves garlic, minced

3 10-ounce packages frozen chopped spinach,
thawed and wrung dry

3 tablespoons nutritional yeast

2 teaspoons dried basil

½ teaspoon dried thyme

½ to 1 teaspoon sea salt, or use more or less
to taste

Black pepper to taste

Preheat the oven to 350 degrees F.

In a large bowl, mash all the tofu until it resembles ricotta cheese. Set aside. Sauté the onion in
a large skillet for 7 to 8 minutes, until it is translucent and starts to brown. Add the garlic and
sauté another minute. Remove from heat and
add to the tofu mixture along with the spinach,
nutritional yeast, basil, thyme, salt, and pepper.
Combine well.

Spicy Seitan

2 shallots, minced

6 cloves garlic, minced

2 teaspoons chili powder

1 teaspoon crushed red pepper

1½ teaspoons ground sage

1½ teaspoons ground fennel

2 18-ounce packages chicken-style seitan (see
   note), coarsely chopped

½ cup water

Sea salt to taste

In a medium skillet, sauté the shallots over
medium heat 3 to 4 minutes. Add water 1 to
2 tablespoons at a time to keep the shallots from
sticking. Add the garlic and spices, and cook for
another minute. Add the seitan and ½ cup water,
and cook until the liquid is reduced by half, about
5 minutes. Season with salt.

Chef's Note • Seitan is a meat substitute made from
wheat gluten and comes in traditional or "beef" or
"chicken" styles.

6

Appetizers

Traditional Low-Fat Hummus

SERVES 4

I've been making hummus one way or another for more than twenty years, and while I still like traditional hummus made with garbanzo beans, I love some of the variations that you can make by changing the beans and adding roasted peppers, spinach, or artichoke hearts. How you make your hummus is up to you, but here is one of six ways in this book to make it kick. This one is traditional (though low in fat!), but try any of the others for an unusual twist on hummus.

2 cups cooked garbanzo beans, warmed

6 cloves garlic, or to taste

3 tablespoons lemon juice

¾ teaspoon ground cumin

Sea salt to taste

Combine all ingredients in a food processor and purée until smooth and creamy. Add water if needed to make a smooth consistency.

Spinach-Wasabi Hummus

SERVES 4 TO 6

Wasabi is a condiment similar to horseradish that is used in Japanese cooking. A little wasabi goes a long way in adding a kick to any dish.

2 cups cooked garbanzo beans, rinsed, drained, and warmed

1 10-ounce package frozen spinach, thawed and wrung dry

4 cloves garlic, minced

Zest of 1 lemon

Juice of 2 lemons

2 teaspoons wasabi powder, or use more or less to taste

Sea salt to taste

Combine all ingredients in a food processor and purée until smooth and creamy.

Artichoke and Basil Hummus

Artichokes and basil raise hummus to new heights.

2 cups cooked garbanzo beans, rinsed, drained,
   and warmed
½ cup fresh basil
4 cloves garlic, minced
Zest and juice of 1 lemon
Sea salt to taste
1 14-ounce can artichoke hearts (about 2 cups),
   drained

Combine the garbanzo beans, basil, garlic, lemon
zest and juice, and salt in a food processor and
purée until smooth and creamy. Add the artichoke hearts and pulse to chop well, leaving the
artichoke hearts chunky.

Fava Bean–Red Pepper Hummus

I stir in the roasted pepper at the end of this recipe so you can taste both the fava bean purée and the red bell pepper distinctly.

2 cups cooked fava beans

4 cloves garlic, minced

Zest of 1 lemon

Sea salt to taste

1 roasted red bell pepper, finely diced

Combine everything but the red bell pepper in a food processor and purée until smooth and creamy. Pour the hummus into a bowl and stir in the diced red bell pepper.

Lemon-Kalamata Hummus

The lemon and olives really give this hummus a kick with a Greek flair. Add a little fresh dill if you like for a truly unusual spread.

2 cups cooked garbanzo beans, rinsed, drained, and warmed

½ cup kalamata olives, pitted and drained

4 cloves garlic, minced

Zest of 2 lemons

Combine all ingredients in a food processor and purée until smooth and creamy.

Cracked Black Pepper Hummus

Freshly cracked black pepper adds bite to any dish, but in this one it takes center stage.

2 cups cooked garbanzo beans, rinsed, drained,
   and warmed
4 cloves garlic, minced
Zest of 1 lemon
Juice of 2 lemons
1 teaspoon fresh cracked black pepper, or use more
   or less to taste
Sea salt to taste

Combine all ingredients in a food processor and purée until smooth and creamy.

White Bean Spread

This Tuscan-inspired spread is a great filling for wraps, or sauce for pizza. I often eat it as a dip for fresh vegetables.

2 cups cooked cannellini beans

4 cloves garlic

Zest and juice of 1 lemon

1 teaspoon minced fresh rosemary

Sea salt and black pepper to taste

Combine all ingredients in a food processor and pulse or purée until smooth. Add water as needed to make a smooth paste.

Chestnut and White Bean Spread

See photo on pages 136–137.

Chestnuts are one of my favorite nuts, not only because they are so low in fat compared to other nuts (one cup of chestnuts has 350 calories and only 27 of them are from fat), but also because they have a great flavor.

1 15.5-ounce can chestnut purée or approximately 2 cups canned whole chestnuts pureéd in a food processor with enough water to make a creamy consistency

1 15-ounce can cannellini beans (about 1¾ cups), rinsed and drained

2 cloves garlic, minced

Zest of 1 lemon

2 teaspoons ground cumin

2 teaspoons dried tarragon

Sea salt to taste

¼ teaspoon cayenne pepper

Combine everything in a food processor and purée until smooth and creamy. Serve with pita, on crackers, or in a wrap with sprouts or spinach.

Chestnut and White Bean Spread (page 135)

White Bean Pesto

A perfect topping for pizza or bruschetta, a great dip for vegetables, or a garnish for soup. For a fat-free version, leave out the pine nuts.

4 cups fresh basil leaves

1 15-ounce can cannellini or other white beans, rinsed and drained

8 cloves garlic, minced

½ cup nutritional yeast

¼ cup toasted pine nuts (optional)

Sea salt to taste

Combine all ingredients in a food processor and blend until smooth and creamy.

Spinach-Artichoke Dip

This unusual twist on a popular party food is delicious and filling, made here with beans instead of the usual sour cream. The beans make it hearty enough to be a filling for wraps and yet creamy enough to be a dip for vegetables or crackers.

1 15-ounce can navy or other white beans, rinsed and drained

1 10-ounce package frozen spinach, thawed and wrung dry

1 14-ounce can artichoke hearts packed in water, drained

6 cloves garlic, minced

¼ cup nutritional yeast

Sea salt to taste

Pinch of ground nutmeg

Purée the beans in a food processor until smooth and creamy. Add the remaining ingredients and pulse-chop to mix well.

Ajvar
(Serbian Red Pepper Spread)

SERVES 4 TO 6

I heard this recipe described on a public radio station one day and knew I had to try it. Every recipe I found had a large quantity of olive oil—so of course I got rid of that and added extra garlic and a little lemon zest to make the flavor pop. Serve this easy-to-make spread on crusty bread or as a filling for a wrap with mixed greens and sprouts or Jicama Slaw (page 256).

1 large eggplant (about 1½ pounds)

4 large red bell peppers

4 cloves garlic, finely chopped

Zest and juice of 1 lemon

Sea salt and black pepper to taste

Preheat the oven to 475 degrees F. Place the eggplant and red bell peppers on a baking sheet and roast them until their skins blister and turn black, about 30 minutes.

Place the peppers in a plastic bag and let them sweat for 15 minutes. Let the eggplant cool, then cut it in half and scoop the flesh into a food

processor. Peel the blackened skin from the peppers, coarsely chop them, and add them to the bowl with the eggplant and the remaining ingredients. Pulse-chop the mixture until it resembles a chunky salsa. Serve at room temperature.

Soups

Basic Soup Stock

Make a quick and satisfying soup by cooking 2 quarts of this with 1½ cups of split peas and a teaspoon of freshly chopped thyme, or 3 large baking potatoes and 1 large onion that has been sautéed in a skillet for 7 or 8 minutes. You can also cook grains with this stock to give them flavor, or use it in a stir-fry for added zing.

2 large leeks, chopped and rinsed

2 stalks celery, including some leaves, coarsely chopped

2 large carrots, peeled and coarsely chopped

1 bunch green onions, chopped

4 cloves garlic, minced

6 sprigs fresh parsley

4 sprigs fresh thyme

2 bay leaves

10 cups water

Add all ingredients to a large pot and bring to a boil over high heat. Decrease the heat to medium and let the pot simmer for 45 minutes. Discard the solids and let the stock cool to room temperature before storing in an airtight container. Refrigerate for up to seven days.

Creole Corn Chowder

SERVES 6

See photo on page 258.

Creole cooking starts with tomatoes, peppers, onions, and celery, and adds a mixture of spices that vary from household to household. You can buy a creole seasoning blend or make your own like the one on page 149.

1 large yellow onion, diced

1 stalk celery, diced

1 large red bell pepper, diced

4 ears corn, kernels removed from the cobs
  (about 3 cups)

1 tablespoon Creole Spice Blend, or use more or
  less to taste (store-bought, or recipe follows)

1 bay leaf

2 cups vegetable stock or Basic Soup Stock
  (page 146)

1 large russet potato, peeled and diced

2 cups Cauliflower Purée (page 72)

2 tablespoons nutritional yeast

Sea salt and black pepper to taste

(continued on following page)

(continued from previous page)

Sauté the onion, celery, and red bell pepper in a large saucepan over medium heat for 7 to 8 minutes. Add water 1 to 2 tablespoons at a time to keep the vegetables from sticking. Add the corn and Creole Spice Blend, and cook for another minute. Add the bay leaf, vegetable stock, and diced potato, and cook, covered, over medium-low heat for 20 minutes, until the potatoes are tender. Add the cauliflower purée, nutritional yeast, and sea salt and pepper to taste, and cook over medium-low heat for another 10 minutes.

Creole Spice Blend

2 tablespoons sweet paprika

1 tablespoon dried oregano

1 tablespoon dried basil

1 tablespoon granulated onion

1 tablespoon granulated garlic

2 teaspoons dried thyme

2 teaspoons cayenne pepper, or use more
    or less to taste

2 teaspoons white pepper, or use more
    or less to taste

1 teaspoon black pepper

Combine everything in a small bowl and mix well. Store in an airtight container for up to three months.

White Gazpacho

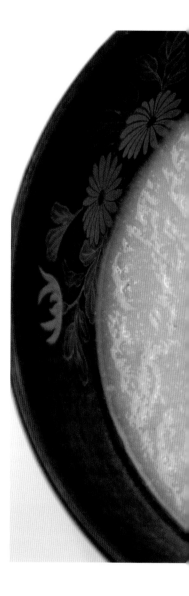

Most variations of this soup have a lot of toasted almonds and some olive oil, making it too fatty a soup for my kitchen. My recipe bumps up the cucumber, gets rid of the oil, and cuts the almonds in half for a tasty low-fat version of an Andalusian classic.

- 2 large cucumbers, peeled, seeded, and chopped (6 cups)
- 1 cup Cauliflower Purée (page 72)
- ½ cup green seedless grapes
- ½ cup diced honeydew melon
- ¼ cup toasted slivered almonds
- ¼ cup chopped white onion
- 2 cloves garlic, minced
- 3 tablespoons brown rice vinegar
- Sea salt and white pepper to taste

Combine all ingredients in a blender and purée until smooth and creamy. Chill until ready to serve.

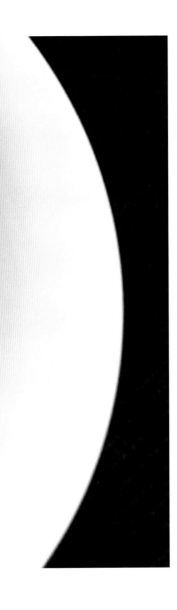

Chilled Tomato Bisque

SERVES 4

I make this easy soup when tomatoes are perfectly ripe in the garden. The cauliflower purée makes this soup creamy without the fat of heavy cream.

2 pounds ripe tomatoes, stems removed and
   coarsely chopped
1 cup Cauliflower Purée (page 72)
2 cloves garlic, minced
2 tablespoons white wine vinegar
Sea salt and black pepper to taste
Almond milk as needed

Combine the first five ingredients in a blender and purée until smooth and creamy. Add almond milk as necessary to achieve a creamy consistency. Serve immediately or chill.

Chilled Sweet Potato Bisque

SERVES 6

I used to go to a Caribbean-inspired restaurant with the most amazing soups, full of flavor. Many of the soups were puréed and I liked to eat them with a loaf of the restaurant's homemade bread. I still like puréed soups but usually eat them over brown rice or some other grain for a healthier meal.

3 large sweet potatoes (about 2½ pounds)

4 cups vegetable stock or Basic Soup Stock (page 146)

1½ cups Best Date Syrup Ever (page 83)

Zest of 1 orange

Juice of 2 oranges

1 teaspoon allspice

1 teaspoon ground ginger

Cayenne pepper to taste

¾ cup unsweetened almond milk

Sea salt to taste

Peel, cube, and steam the sweet potatoes until very tender, about 12 minutes. Purée the potatoes with the vegetable stock until smooth and creamy. Add the purée to a pot with the date syrup, orange zest and juice, allspice, ginger, and cayenne pepper. Bring the mixture to a simmer and let it cook for 15 minutes. Add the almond milk and salt to taste, and chill until ready to serve, about 2 hours.

Cream of Mushroom Soup

See photo on pages 158–159.

I like my soups thick and hearty, or smooth and creamy, and full of flavor—brothy soups are not my thing. That's probably because I like dipping things in my soup: bread, crackers, tortillas, whatever. I also like to use soups like this one to serve as a sauce over baked potatoes, pasta, or plain brown rice—delicious!

1 ounce porcini mushrooms (about 1 cup), steeped
   in 1 cup hot water for 30 minutes
1 pound cremini or button mushrooms
   (about 5 cups), cleaned and sliced
1 large leek, white and light green parts only, diced
1 medium shallot, diced small
½ cup dry white wine
1 small bay leaf
1 teaspoon minced fresh thyme
2 cups Cauliflower Purée (page 72)

4 cups vegetable stock or Basic Soup Stock
(page 146)

Sea salt and black pepper to taste

Remove the porcini mushrooms from the steeping liquid and coarsely chop them. Reserve the liquid. Add the porcini mushrooms to a large saucepan with the cremini or button mushrooms, leek, and shallot. Sauté over medium heat for 8 to 10 minutes. Add water 1 to 2 tablespoons at a time to keep the vegetables from sticking. Add the wine, bay leaf, thyme, and ½ cup of the porcini-steeped liquid, and cook until the liquid is almost evaporated. Add the cauliflower purée and vegetable stock, and cook for 10 minutes. Season with salt and pepper.

Cream of Mushroom Soup (page 156)

Turkish Red Lentil Soup

I have eaten several varities of this delicious soup. One of my favorites was in a Turkish restaurant in Bloomington, Indiana, called Anatolia. The simple but flavorful blend of lemon and mint is very well balanced and very satisfying. Here is my version of that soup.

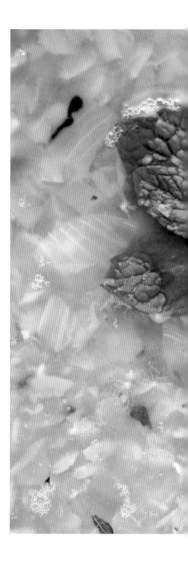

1 medium onion, finely diced

3 cloves garlic, minced

2 cups dried red lentils

8 cups vegetable stock or Basic Soup Stock
   (page 146)

Zest and juice of 1 lemon

1 tablespoon dried mint

Sea salt to taste

Pinch of cayenne pepper

Sauté the onion over medium heat for 8 to 10 minutes, until translucent and starting to brown. Add water 1 to 2 tablespoons at a time to keep them from sticking. Add the garlic and cook for another minute, then add the lentils and

vegetable stock. Bring to a boil over high heat. Decrease the heat to medium and cook, covered, for 25 minutes. When the lentils are tender and have started to break down, add the lemon zest and juice, mint, salt, and cayenne pepper. Let cook for another 5 minutes.

Succotash Soup

I've made this with lima beans and edamame and I like it either way. In the warm summer months, the edamame is a little lighter.

3 large leeks, white and light green parts only,
  diced into ½-inch cubes
1 large red bell pepper, diced into ½-inch cubes
3 cloves garlic, minced
2 teaspoons dried thyme
6 cups vegetable stock or Basic Soup Stock
  (page 146)
1 10-ounce package frozen edamame, shelled
4 cups fresh corn or 2 10-ounce packages
  frozen corn
½ cup chopped fresh basil
Sea salt and black pepper to taste

Heat a large pot over medium heat. Add the leeks and red bell pepper and cook for 7 to 8 minutes, until the leeks start to brown and turn translucent. Add water 1 to 2 tablespoons at a time to keep the vegetables from sticking. Add the garlic and thyme and sauté for 1 minute. Add the vegetable stock, edamame, and corn, and bring to a boil. Decrease heat to medium-low, cover, and simmer for 20 to 25 minutes. Add the chopped basil and cook for another minute. Remove the soup from heat and season to taste with salt and pepper.

Spicy Black Bean–Sweet Potato Stew

SERVES 8

The sweet potatoes and cinnamon counterbalance this hearty, savory stew nicely.

1 large onion, diced

3 cloves garlic, minced

2 teaspoons ground cumin

1 teaspoon ground cinnamon

2 teaspoons ground coriander

Zest of 1 orange

2 large sweet potatoes, peeled and chopped

4 cups cooked black beans

3 cups vegetable stock or Basic Soup Stock
    (page 146)

1 28-ounce can diced tomatoes

Sea salt and black pepper to taste

1 cup chopped fresh cilantro (garnish)

2 jalapeño peppers, seeded and finely chopped
    (garnish)

2 fresh limes, quartered (garnish)

Sauté the onion in a large saucepan over medium-high heat for 7 to 8 minutes. Add water 1 to 2 tablespoons at a time to keep the onion

from sticking. Add the garlic, cumin, cinnamon, coriander, and orange zest. Sauté for 1 minute. Add the sweet potatoes, black beans, and vegetable stock. Bring to a boil, decrease heat, and simmer for 15 minutes, until the sweet potatoes are tender. Add the tomatoes and more stock if needed, and cook for another 10 minutes. Season with salt and pepper and cook for 5 minutes. Serve garnished with the chopped cilantro and jalapeño peppers, with lime wedges on the side.

Smoky Black Bean Bisque

SERVES 4

I'm never afraid to take one recipe and find a few uses for it. This soup is a good example of that. It's great as is or served with a few fresh garnishes, as a topping for baked potatoes, or as a gravy for veggies and rice.

1 small yellow onion, diced small

2 cloves garlic, minced

2 teaspoons cumin seeds, toasted and ground

2 teaspoons minced fresh oregano

3 chipotle peppers in adobo sauce

4 cups cooked black beans

2½ to 3 cups vegetable stock or Basic Soup Stock (page 146)

Sea salt to taste

1 lime, quartered (garnish)

1 cup finely chopped fresh cilantro (garnish)

1 small red onion, diced small (garnish)

Sauté the yellow onion in a stockpot over medium heat for 8 minutes. Add water 1 to 2 tablespoons at a time to keep the onion from sticking. Add the garlic, cumin, and oregano, and cook for another minute. Add the chipotles, black beans, and vegetable stock, and bring to a boil over high heat. Decrease the heat to medium and cook the soup, covered, for 20 minutes. Season with salt and purée the soup in batches in a blender. Return the puréed soup to a pot and keep warm. Serve garnished with the lime wedges, cilantro, and red onion.

Watercress-Potato Soup

A simple but delicious soup with a little bit of a kick from the peppery watercress. If you can't find watercress in the store, you can use a single bunch of chopped mustard greens.

2 large leeks, diced

3 cloves garlic, minced

1 teaspoon minced fresh thyme

4 large potatoes, peeled and diced

5 cups vegetable stock or Basic Soup Stock
   (page 146)

2 bunches watercress, chopped

Sea salt and pepper to taste

Sauté the leeks in a large saucepan over medium heat until softened, about 8 minutes. Add water 1 to 2 tablespoons at a time to keep them from sticking. Add the garlic and thyme, and cook for 2 minutes. Add the potatoes and vegetable stock, and bring to a boil. Cover the pot, decrease the heat to medium, and cook until the potatoes are tender, about 20 minutes. Add the watercress and cook for 5 minutes. Purée the soup in batches in a blender and return to a pan over low heat. Season with salt and pepper and cook for another 5 minutes.

Southwestern Corn and Potato Soup

This is one of my favorite soups, but when I want a change I make it with 1 tablespoon of curry powder instead of the ground cumin—just to shake things up.

1 large yellow onion, diced into ¼-inch cubes

1 large red bell pepper, diced into ¼-inch cubes

4 ears corn, kernels removed from the cobs
  (about 3 cups)

3 cloves garlic, minced

2 teaspoons cumin seeds, toasted and ground

2 jalapeño peppers, minced

½ cup finely chopped fresh cilantro

6 cups vegetable stock or Basic Soup Stock
  (page 146)

2 large potatoes, cut into ¼-inch pieces

Sea salt and black pepper to taste

Sauté the onion and red bell pepper over medium heat for 7 to 8 minutes. Add water 1 to 2 tablespoons at a time to keep the vegetables from sticking. Add the corn, garlic, cumin, jalapeño peppers, and cilantro, and cook for 2 minutes. Add the vegetable stock and potatoes, and bring the pot to a boil. Cook for 15 minutes or so, until the potatoes are tender. Add salt and pepper to taste, and cook for a few minutes more.

8

Wraps, Sandwiches, Pizza, and Flatbreads

Zucchini Pritti–Hummus Wrap

SERVES 4

I'm always looking for new fillings for wraps and ways to make hummus a little more exciting. Sometimes I make a simple stir-fry and add it to a wrap with some kind of spread—usually hummus—and sometimes I'll use a leftover side dish to add to my usual filling. Zucchini Pritti, an Israeli dish, is a great example of one of those recipes that make good use of the leftovers. I cook the zucchini oil-free with a little onion and then sauté the remaining ingredients to serve on top.

3 large zucchini, sliced ½ inch thick

2 medium yellow onions, diced and divided

Sea salt and pepper to taste

1 medium green bell pepper, diced

1 medium tomato, diced

2 cups Traditional Low-Fat Hummus (page 128)

Sea salt and black pepper to taste

4 10- or 12-inch whole-wheat tortillas

4 green onions, thinly sliced

(continued on following page)

(continued from previous page)

Sauté the zucchini and half of the onions in a medium saucepan over medium-high heat for 6 to 7 minutes, until the onions start to turn translucent and the zucchini start to brown. Add water 1 to 2 tablespoons at a time to keep the vegetables from sticking. Season the vegetables with salt and pepper, and remove from the pan; set them aside. Sauté the remaining onion and the green bell pepper over medium-high heat for 5 minutes. Add the tomato and cook for 5 minutes more. Season with salt and pepper and pour over the zucchini.

To make the wraps, divide the hummus evenly between the four whole-wheat tortillas and spoon the vegetables over the hummus. Sprinkle the green onions over the vegetables and roll each tortilla up around the filling.

Portobello Wraps with Spicy Asian Slaw

SERVES 4

This is one of my favorite lunches. Sometime I grill
the mushrooms whole and make a burger out of it,
but usually I eat it like this.

½ cup rice wine vinegar

¼ cup brown rice syrup

1 tablespoon low-sodium soy sauce

4 cups coleslaw mix

½ red bell pepper, diced small

1 large jalapeño pepper, minced

½ cup chopped green onions

½ cup chopped fresh cilantro

4 medium portobello mushrooms,
   sliced ½ inch thick

1 medium yellow onion, cut into ½-inch slivers

Sea salt and black pepper to taste

4 10- or 12-inch whole-grain tortillas

(continued on following page)

(continued from previous page)

Combine the vinegar, rice syrup, and soy sauce in a medium bowl. Add the coleslaw mix, red bell pepper, jalapeño pepper, green onions, and cilantro, and mix well. Let sit for 30 minutes before serving.

Heat a large skillet over medium-high heat. Add the mushrooms and yellow onion, and cook, stirring frequently, for 7 to 8 minutes, until the vegetables are tender. Season with salt and pepper and set aside.

To make the wraps, lay each tortilla flat on a surface and divide the mushrooms between them. Spoon some of the slaw over the mushrooms and roll each tortilla up.

Chef's Note • If your tortilla does not roll without cracking, warm it in a dry skillet over medium heat for a few minutes to soften it.

Black Bean Burritos

See photo on pages 74–75.

You can make almost any bean dish into burritos, but only this one comes with a chipotle cream sauce.

1 large yellow onion, diced

1 large red bell pepper, diced

3 cups cooked black beans

4 cloves garlic, minced

1½ tablespoons ground cumin

3 tablespoons lime juice

¾ cup chopped fresh cilantro

Sea salt and black pepper

4 10- or 12-inch whole-wheat tortillas

1 cup Chipotle Cream Sauce (page 76)

Sauté the onion and red bell pepper over medium heat for 7 to 8 minutes, until tender. Add water 1 to 2 tablespoons at a time to keep the veggies from sticking. Add the black beans, garlic, cumin, lime juice, and cilantro. Season with salt and pepper.

Divide the bean and vegetable mixture between the four tortillas and spread the chipotle cream over it. Fold the top of each tortilla over the veggies and then fold the sides in toward the center of the wrap and roll it up like a cigar.

White Bean Veggie Wrap

SERVES 4

See photo on pages 182–183.

This is my go-to summer veggie dinner. Yum!

1 red onion, diced

1 red bell pepper, diced

1 medium zucchini, diced

1 medium yellow squash, diced

Sea salt and black pepper to taste

4 12-inch whole-grain flatbreads

1 cup White Bean Spread (page 134) or hummus

½ cup chopped fresh basil

Heat a large skillet over high heat. Add the onion, red bell pepper, zucchini, and yellow squash, and stir-fry until the onion is translucent and the vegetables start to brown, about 5 to 6 minutes. Add water 1 to 2 tablespoons at a time to keep the vegetables from sticking. Season with salt and pepper. Set aside while you prepare the remaining ingredients.

Spread each flatbread with ¼ cup white bean spread or hummus. Top with sautéed vegetables and some of the chopped basil. Fold in the top half of one flatbread over the vegetable mixture, fold in the sides, and roll the wrap up like a cigar. Repeat with the remaining flatbreads.

White Bean Veggie Wrap (page 181)

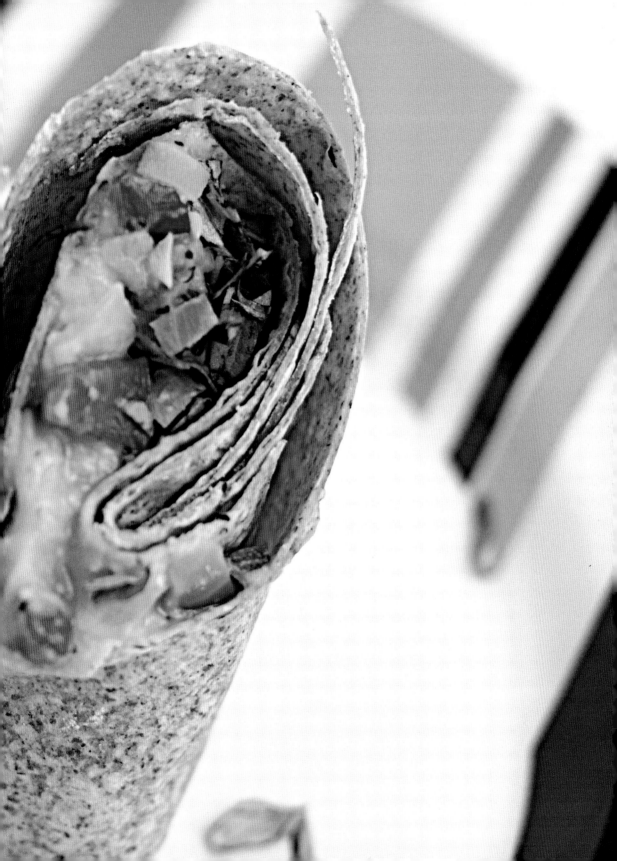

Hot and Sour Ratatouille Calzones with White Bean Pesto

SERVES 3 TO 4

Replace the traditional ratatouille with my hot and sour version and replace traditional basil pesto with cilantro pesto, and you have a delicious East-meets-West version of this popular Italian street food.

1 recipe Whole-Wheat Pizza Dough (page 186)

1 cup White Bean Pesto (page 138), made with cilantro instead of basil

3 cups Hot and Sour Eggplant Ratatouille (page 240)

2 tablespoons cornmeal

Preheat the oven to 425 degrees F. Divide the dough into four pieces and shape each piece into a 6-inch round. Spread pesto over the dough and ¾ cup ratatouille in the center of the dough. Fold the dough over the ratatouille and press the ends together to seal. Place on a cornmeal-dusted baking sheet and let sit for 10 minutes. Bake for 13 to 15 minutes.

Whole-Wheat Pizza Dough

Friday nights used to be pizza nights in my house. I would make my own pizza dough and homemade tempeh sausage, seasoned with fennel, sage, and lots of garlic. Of course the sausage was made with plenty of oil and the pizza was topped with plenty of cheese. I still make pizza on occasion, but these days I skip the cheese—even vegan cheeses are full of fat—and no oil touches my pizza. I also make a thin crust to cut back on the extra calories that a thicker crust can add.

1 envelope active dry baking yeast
1 tablespoon cane sugar
1 cup warm water (about 110 degrees F)
½ teaspoon sea salt
About 2 cups whole-wheat bread flour

Add the yeast and sugar to the warm water and whisk them together. Let the mixture sit until it starts to foam, then add the salt and, using a whisk, stir in 1 cup of the flour. Beat the dough for

75 strokes. Add as much of the remaining flour as needed to make a dough that is stiff but still a little tacky to the touch. Cover the dough with plastic wrap and let it sit in a warm place until it has doubled in volume, about 45 minutes. Punch it down and let it rise again, about 20 minutes. Divide the dough into two pieces and shape into two round, flat crusts. Use in any recipe that calls for whole-wheat pizza dough or crust, following the recipe's topping and baking instructions.

Red, White, and Green Pizza

SERVES 2 TO 4

This is the perfect pizza to make when zucchini, tomatoes, and basil are ripe in the garden. The creamy leek sauce is light yet full of flavor and does not overwhelm the toppings.

2 tablespoons cornmeal

1 recipe Whole-Wheat Pizza Dough (page 186)

½ cup Creamy Leek Sauce (page 79)

1 medium zucchini, diced

½ pint cherry tomatoes, halved

½ medium red onion, diced

Sea salt and pepper to taste

½ cup chopped fresh basil

Preheat the oven to 425 degrees F. Dust a 12-inch pizza pan or baking sheet with cornmeal and press the pizza dough onto the pan or baking sheet. Spread the leek sauce over the dough and distribute the zucchini, cherry tomatoes, and red onion over it. Season with salt and pepper. Bake for 12 to 13 minutes, until the crust is browned. Remove the pizza from the oven and sprinkle the chopped basil over it.

Sun-Dried Tomato Pesto Flatbread

SERVES 2 TO 4

Sun-dried tomato pesto is a great base for many flatbreads. If you are buying store-bought pizza dough, watch out for the added oil. If you can't find one without the added fat, then make my Whole-Wheat Pizza Dough (page 186).

2 large onions, thinly sliced

1 cup sun-dried tomatoes steeped in warm water for 30 minutes, until soft

4 cloves garlic, minced

Sea salt and freshly ground black pepper

1 cup (packed) fresh basil

½ cup nutritional yeast

2 tablespoons cornmeal

1 recipe Whole-Wheat Pizza Dough (page 186)

1 cup thinly sliced button mushrooms

1 small zucchini, thinly sliced

Preheat the oven to 425 degrees F.

Sauté the onions in a large skillet over medium heat for 12 to 15 minutes, until they are well browned. Add water as needed to keep them from sticking to the pan. Set them aside while you prepare the rest of the dish.

To make the pesto, blend the rehydrated sun-dried tomatoes, garlic, salt and pepper, and basil in a food processor and process until the tomatoes are finely chopped. Transfer the tomato mixture to a large bowl. Stir in the nutritional yeast.

Dust a 12-inch pizza pan or baking sheet with cornmeal and press the pizza dough onto the pan or baking sheet. Spread the pesto over the dough and top with the vegetables. Bake for 12 to 15 minutes, until the crust is browned. Let cool for a few minutes before cutting.

Hummus, Pesto, and Tomato Flatbread

SERVES 2 TO 4

Hummus makes a great sauce for pizza, and hummus and pesto come together nicely either on pizza or in a wrap.

2 tablespoons cornmeal

1 recipe Whole-Wheat Pizza Dough (page 186)

1 cup Traditional Low-Fat Hummus (page 128)

2 large tomatoes, thinly sliced

½ cup White Bean Pesto (page 138)

Sea salt and pepper to taste

Preheat the oven to 425 degrees F. Dust a 12-inch pizza pan or baking sheet with cornmeal and press the pizza dough onto the pan or baking sheet. Spread the hummus over the unbaked crust. Layer the tomatoes on top, covering the hummus completely. Drop dollops of pesto on top of the tomatoes. Season with salt and pepper. Bake for 12 to 13 minutes, until the crust is browned.

Southwestern Black Bean and Pesto Flatbread

SERVES 2 TO 4

I usually keep some kind of pesto on hand. I use cilantro in the spring when it is fresh in the garden. Later in the summer when I have more basil than I can manage, I make much of it into pesto to freeze. And of course when corn is at its best in August, I find as many uses for it as I can, mostly eating it off the cob, but also on a hearty pizza like this one.

2 tablespoons cornmeal

1 recipe Whole-Wheat Pizza Dough (page 186)

½ cup White Bean Pesto (page 138), made with
   cilantro instead of basil

1 medium tomato, chopped

2 ears corn, kernels removed from the cobs, or
   ¾ cup frozen corn

½ roasted red pepper, chopped

½ cup cooked black beans

Sea salt and pepper to taste

Preheat the oven to 425 degrees F. Dust a 12-inch pizza pan or baking sheet with cornmeal and press the pizza dough onto the pan or baking

sheet. Spread the pesto over the unbaked crust
and distribute the remaining toppings over it.
Season with salt and pepper. Bake for 12 to
13 minutes, until the crust is browned.

Smoky Black Bean Flatbread

Black beans puréed with chipotles in adobo sauce make a great sauce for pizza. If you don't like the spicy hot chiles, you could soak an ancho chile in warm water for 30 minutes. Seed it and purée it with the black beans. It will give you the smoky flavor without the heat.

Pickled Red Onions

½ cup brown rice vinegar

2 tablespoons brown rice syrup

1½ teaspoons sea salt

2 whole cloves, lightly crushed

1 medium red onion, thinly sliced

2 tablespoons cornmeal

1 cup cooked black beans

2 to 3 chipotle peppers in adobo sauce

½ teaspoon sea salt

1 recipe Whole-Wheat Pizza Dough (page 186)

1 cup cherry tomatoes, halved

½ small yellow pepper, diced

½ cup chopped fresh cilantro (garnish)

To prepare the pickled onions, combine the brown rice vinegar, brown rice syrup, salt, crushed cloves, and red onion in a jar with a tight-fitting lid and shake vigorously until the salt has dissolved. Let sit for 1 hour before using.

Preheat the oven to 425 degrees F. Dust a 12-inch pizza pan or baking sheet with cornmeal. Purée the black beans, chipotle peppers, and salt in a food processor. Add enough water to make a pourable sauce. Spread the sauce over the pizza dough and arrange the pickled onions, cherry tomatoes, and yellow peppers over the sauce. Place the pizza on the prepared pan or baking sheet and bake for 12 to 13 minutes. Garnish the pizza with the chopped cilantro.

Entrées

Tropical "Chicken" Salad

This is one of my favorite summer dinners. The fresh fruits and vegetables come together nicely in a sweet and savory dressing.

Zest and juice of 2 limes

¼ cup low-sodium soy sauce

⅓ cup Best Date Syrup Ever (page 83)

2 tablespoons brown rice vinegar

1 18-ounce package chicken-style seitan, coarsely chopped

1 red bell pepper, diced

2 mangoes, peeled, seeded, and diced into ½-inch cubes

½ fresh pineapple, peeled, cored, and cubed

2 cups mung bean sprouts

½ bunch green onions, finely sliced on a diagonal

½ bunch fresh cilantro, chopped

Combine the zest and lime juice, soy sauce, and date syrup, and set aside. Combine the remaining ingredients in a large bowl and toss together with the lime mixture. Refrigerate for 30 minutes.

Gado Gado

VARIES

This popular Indonesian vegetable dish can be made with any number of vegetables. Choose your preferred veggies or try my favorite version with steamed broccoli, sweet potatoes, beets, and arugula. You will need about 4 cups of vegetables and ¼ cup Ginger-Miso Dressing (page 95) per serving to make this dish a meal. This dish is often served with a spicy peanut sauce. To cut the fat, I make it with a ginger-miso dressing without sacrificing any of the flavor.

Cooked Vegetables

Blanched or steamed vegetables (green beans, cauliflower, broccoli, etc.)

Sweet potatoes, peeled, cubed, and steamed until tender, about 8 minutes

Beets, peeled, thinly sliced, and steamed until tender, about 6 minutes

Fresh Vegetables

Chinese cabbage, shredded

Carrots, peeled and thinly sliced

Lettuce, spinach, arugula, or mixed greens

Tomato wedges

Cucumber slices

Ginger-Miso Dressing (page 95)

Arrange all of the vegetables on a large platter
and spoon the dressing over them.

Black Bean Burgers

See photo on page 250.

I make a large batch of these and freeze them to have on hand for a quick meal. My favorite way to garnish them is with lettuce, sliced tomatoes, and spicy Jalapeño Mayonnaise (page 86), or with Spicy Asian Slaw (page 254).

2 cups cooked black beans

3 tablespoons arrowroot powder

2 teaspoons ancho chili powder

2 cloves garlic, minced

2 teaspoons cumin seeds, toasted and ground

½ teaspoon sea salt

1 small red onion, diced small

1 jalapeño pepper, minced

¼ cup cornmeal

4 whole-grain buns

4 leaves green leaf lettuce

1 large tomato, sliced

½ cup Jalapeño Mayonnaise (page 86)

Place the black beans in a bowl and coarsely mash them. Add the arrowroot powder, chili powder, garlic, cumin, salt, red onion, and jalapeño pepper. Mix well. Shape the bean mixture into four patties and gently toss each one into the cornmeal. Place them on a parchment-lined baking sheet and refrigerate them for 1 hour.

Preheat the oven to 375 degrees F. Bake the burgers for 20 minutes, gently turn them over, and bake for another 20 minutes. Serve the burgers on whole-grain buns with lettuce, tomato, and a dollop of jalapeño mayonnaise.

Scalloped Potatoes

This version of one of my childhood favorite dishes has all of the flavor but none of the fat of the one my mom used to make. And while health influences the ingredients in my scalloped potatoes, my mom is the influence behind the great taste. Thanks, Mom.

4 pounds russet potatoes, thinly sliced

2 cups Cauliflower Purée (page 72)

½ cup vegetable stock or Basic Soup Stock
   (page 146)

¼ cup nutritional yeast

1 clove garlic, minced

Sea salt and black pepper to taste

¼ teaspoon freshly grated nutmeg

Preheat the oven to 375 degrees F. Steam the potatoes for 5 minutes or so, until just tender. Set them aside while you prepare the sauce.

Combine all the remaining ingredients in a bowl and mix well. Add the potatoes to the bowl and toss to combine. Spread the mixture in a 9 × 13 inch baking dish and cover with foil. Bake for 50 minutes, until the potatoes are tender when poked with a fork. Remove the foil and let the dish cook for another 10 minutes.

Mushroom Tacos with Chipotle Cream

SERVES 4

The earthy mushrooms and the spicy cream sauce wrapped in a corn tortilla make this one of my favorite tacos.

1 medium red onion, thinly sliced

4 large portobello mushrooms, diced into ½-inch cubes

6 cloves garlic, minced

Sea salt to taste

12 6-inch corn tortillas

1 cup Chipotle Cream Sauce (page 76)

2 cups shredded romaine lettuce

½ cup chopped fresh cilantro

Heat a large skillet over medium-high heat. Add the red onion and portobello mushrooms, and stir-fry for 4 to 5 minutes. Add water 1 to 2 table-spoons at a time to keep the onion and mush-rooms from sticking. Add the garlic and cook for 1 minute. Season with salt. While the mushrooms cook, add 4 tortillas to a nonstick skillet and heat them for a few minutes until they soften. Turn them over and heat for 2 minutes more. Remove

them from the pan and set them aside. Repeat with the remaining tortillas.

To serve, divide the cooked mushrooms between the corn tortillas and top with some of the chipotle cream sauce, lettuce, and cilantro.

Sweet Potato–Black Bean Enchiladas

See photo on pages 212–213.

These are my favorite enchiladas. The very versatile sweet potato goes south of the border with some unusual spices like cinnamon and allspice.

1 medium yellow onion, diced small

1 medium sweet potato (about ½ pound), peeled and diced small

4 cloves garlic, minced

1 jalapeño pepper, minced

1 teaspoon ancho chili powder

½ teaspoon ground cinnamon

¼ teaspoon allspice

½ teaspoon ground cumin

Zest and juice of 1 lime

2 cups cooked black beans

Sea salt and black pepper to taste

12 6-inch corn tortillas

3 cups Chili Gravy (page 101)

½ cup chopped green onions (garnish)

Preheat the oven to 350 degrees F.

Sauté the onion in a large skillet for 5 minutes, adding water 1 to 2 tablespoons at a time to keep the onion from sticking. Add the sweet potato and ¼ cup water. Cover and cook over medium-low heat until the potatoes are tender, about 7 or 8 minutes. Remove the cover and let the water evaporate from the pan. Add the garlic, jalapeño pepper, and spices, and cook for 2 minutes. Add the lime zest and juice and black beans, season with salt and pepper, and cook for 5 minutes longer.

Heat another large skillet over medium heat. Add 4 tortillas to the pan and heat them a few minutes until they soften. Turn them over and heat 2 minutes more. Remove them from the pan and set them aside. Repeat with the remaining tortillas.

To make the enchiladas, spoon ¾ cup of the chili gravy on the bottom of a 9 × 13 inch baking dish. Spoon a heaping ¼ cup of the black bean mixture down the center of each tortilla. Roll the tortillas up and place them in the baking dish, seam side down. Cover with the remaining gravy and bake for 20 minutes. Serve garnished with the chopped green onions.

Sweet Potato–Black Bean
Enchiladas (page 210)

Three Sisters Enchiladas

"Three Sisters" refers to the three primary crops in Native American agriculture: maize (or corn), squash, and beans. Cooked simply with garlic, cumin, and chili powder, these three vegetables are simply delicious together and go well in any number of recipes. Here is one of my favorite ways to prepare them.

1 small yellow onion, diced

1 medium butternut squash, peeled and diced into ¼-inch cubes

2 cups corn kernels (about 3 ears) or 1 10-ounce package frozen corn

2 cups cooked pinto beans

4 cloves garlic, minced

½ tablespoon ground cumin

2 teaspoons ancho chili powder

Sea salt to taste

16 6-inch corn tortillas

3 cups Chili Gravy (page 101)

Preheat the oven to 350 degrees F.

Sauté the onion in a large skillet over medium heat for 7 to 8 minutes. Add water 1 to

2 tablespoons at a time to keep onion from sticking. Add the squash and cook for 5 minutes, until it is tender but not mushy. Add the corn, pinto beans, garlic, cumin, and chili powder, and cook for 3 minutes. Season with salt.

Spoon ⅓ cup of the filling down the middle of a corn tortilla and roll the tortilla up over the filling. Place the enchilada, seam side down, in a 9 × 13 inch nonstick baking dish. Repeat with the remaining filling for all the tortillas.

Top the enchiladas with the chili gravy, spreading it to cover the enchiladas, and bake, covered, for 15 minutes. Uncover and bake for another 10 minutes.

Adzuki Bean Tacos

SERVES 4

Adzuki beans taste a little like black-eyed peas. Their sweetness makes them a versatile bean that you can use in any number of dishes. They are one of my favorite beans, and this recipe is one of the ways I like to eat them most. The tangy slaw provides great contrast to the sweetness of the beans.

1 medium onion, minced

1 jalapeño pepper, minced

2 cloves garlic, minced

1 large tomato, diced

2 teaspoons cumin seeds, toasted and ground

2 teaspoons ancho chili powder

Sea salt to taste

Cayenne pepper to taste

2 cups cooked adzuki beans

8 6-inch corn tortillas or taco shells

4 cups Cilantro-Lime Slaw (page 255)

Sauté the onion over medium heat for 6 to 7 minutes. Add the jalapeño pepper, garlic, tomato, cumin, chili powder, salt, and cayenne pepper. Let cook for 10 minutes, then add the beans and cook for another 5 minutes or so, until heated through.

To serve, spoon some of the bean mixture down the center of a tortilla and top with some of the slaw. Repeat with remaining tortillas.

Bangkok Noodles

I love Asian noodle dishes of all kinds. Most are full of fat, so I rarely order them at a restaurant. When I make my own, I replace the high-fat coconut milk with cauliflower purée and a little coconut extract. No one knows the difference.

1 medium yellow onion, cut into ½-inch julienne

2 small hot green chiles (or use more or less to taste), minced

1 large tomato, diced small

4 cloves garlic, minced

2 tablespoons minced fresh ginger

2 cups vegetable stock or Basic Soup Stock (page 146)

1½ cups Cauliflower Purée (page 72) mixed with ½ teaspoon coconut extract

3 tablespoons Thai red curry paste

1½ tablespoons low-sodium soy sauce

4 cups fresh baby spinach

2 cups mung bean sprouts

12 ounces brown rice noodles, cooked according to package instructions

Sea salt and black pepper to taste

1 small bunch cilantro, chopped

Sauté the onion and chiles in a large skillet over medium-high heat for 5 minutes. Add water 1 to 2 tablespoons at a time to keep the vegetables from sticking. Add the tomato, garlic, and ginger, and cook for 2 minutes, then add the vegetable stock and cauliflower purée mixture.

Whisk the red curry paste together in a bowl with some of the liquid from the pan and add the mixture back to the pan. Bring the sauce to a boil and add the soy sauce, spinach, mung bean sprouts, and cooked noodles. Let it cook until the spinach wilts. Season with salt and pepper and serve garnished with the chopped cilantro.

Summer Pasta with Veggies and "Cream"

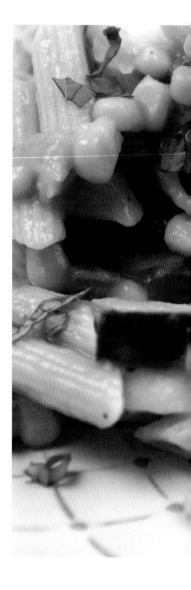

Whole-grain pasta tastes delicious with color-ful summer vegetables, fresh basil, and a creamy sauce. When pasta is a little too heavy for my mood, I replace it with cooked brown rice for a nice change.

- 1 medium yellow onion, diced small
- 1 red bell pepper, diced small
- 2 ears corn, kernels removed from the cobs
- 1 medium zucchini, diced small
- 3 cloves garlic, minced
- Sea salt and black pepper to taste
- 2 cups Cauliflower Purée (page 72)
- 12 ounces whole-grain rotini, cooked according to package instructions
- ½ cup finely chopped fresh basil

Sauté the onion, red bell pepper, and corn in a large saucepan over medium-high heat for 5 minutes. Add water 1 to 2 tablespoons at a time to keep the vegetables from sticking. Add the zucchini and cook for another 4 to 5 minutes. Add

the garlic and cook for another minute. Season with salt and pepper and add the cauliflower purée, cooked pasta, and fresh basil. Cook until the sauce is heated. Season with more salt to taste if desired.

Gnocchi

I love gnocchi. They require a little effort, but they're well worth it. I usually serve them with a red sauce, but occasionally I like them tossed with caramelized onions and some salt and pepper.

2 pounds russet potatoes, peeled and chopped

Sea salt to taste

3 large onions, thinly sliced

1 cup whole-wheat pastry flour

8 teaspoons arrowroot powder

Add the potatoes and 1 quart of water to a large pot. Bring the pot to a boil and cook over medium heat until the potatoes are tender. Drain all but ¼ cup of the cooking water from the pan and mash the potatoes. Season with salt and let cool to almost room temperature.

Sauté the onions in a medium skillet until well caramelized, about 12 minutes. Add water 1 to 2 tablespoons at a time to keep them from sticking. Set them aside.

Sprinkle the flour and arrowroot powder over the potatoes and, working as gently as possible, knead the mixture into a dough. Do not overmix.

If the dough is too sticky, add a little more flour to it. Shape the dough by rolling it into long ropes (you can do this in batches) and then cutting the rope into ¾-inch pieces. Shape each piece by pressing it up against the tines of a fork and flicking it off.

Bring a large pot of salted water to a boil and add the gnocchi to it. Cook until the gnocchi float to the top. Drain and toss with the caramelized onions.

Pasta with Curried Squash Sauce

Puréed vegetables make great sauces. They are flavorful and don't need much else to make them taste good. This one gets a little help from just the right amount of curry powder.

¾ pound butternut squash, halved and seeded

1 pound whole-grain spaghetti or other pasta

½ medium yellow onion, diced

2 cloves garlic, minced

1 tablespoon curry powder

1 teaspoon crushed red pepper (optional)

1½ cups vegetable stock or Basic Soup Stock
    (page 146), plus more as needed

Sea salt to taste

½ cup chopped fresh cilantro

Preheat the oven to 350 degrees F. Place the squash cut side down on a baking sheet and bake it until tender, about 40 to 50 minutes. Remove the squash from the oven and let it cool enough to handle. Scoop the flesh from the skin and purée it in a food processor.

Bring a large pot of salted water to a boil. Add the pasta and cook to al dente, about 8 to 9 minutes, depending on the type of pasta you use.

While the pasta cooks, sauté the onion in a large saucepan for 8 to 10 minutes, until it is tender and starts to brown. Add water 1 to 2 tablespoons at a time to keep it from sticking. Add the garlic and cook for 1 minute, then add the curry powder and crushed red pepper, if using, and cook for another minute. Add the vegetable stock and puréed squash. Whisk the mixture together and simmer for 4 to 5 minutes. Add more vegetable stock if needed to get a creamy consistency. Season with salt.

Drain cooked pasta and add it to the sauce. Mix well. Serve garnished with the chopped cilantro.

Creamy Pasta
and Broccoli

I am happy to eat broccoli steamed with a little salt and pepper, in a stir-fry, or in a creamy sauce like this one. The sauce takes a little effort but don't skip anything; you'll be happy with the results.

12 ounces whole-grain penne pasta

1 head broccoli, cut into florets

2 large leeks, thinly sliced

½ cup white wine

2 cups Cauliflower Purée (page 72)

2 tablespoons nutritional yeast

2 teaspoons Dijon mustard

Zest of 1 lemon

Pinch of ground nutmeg

Sea salt and black pepper to taste

Cook the pasta according to package instructions. Add the broccoli to the pot of pasta in the last 4 minutes of cooking.

While the pasta and broccoli cook, sauté the leeks in a large skillet until they are tender, about 7 to 8 minutes. Add water 1 to 2 tablespoons at a

time to keep the leeks from sticking. Turn the heat up to high, add the wine, and cook until the liquid is reduced by half. Add the cauliflower purée, nutritional yeast, Dijon mustard, lemon zest, and nutmeg. Add salt and pepper to taste.

While the sauce is reducing, drain the cooked pasta and broccoli. Before serving, toss with the sauce.

Penne with Mushrooms and Peas

SERVES 4

I love pasta with creamy sauces and make a lot of them. I do so without guilt when I make a sauce like this one that has no added fat but all of the flavor of a traditional cream-based sauce.

½ ounce dried porcini mushrooms, soaked in 1 cup warm water for 30 minutes

1 large shallot, diced small

1 8-ounce package sliced mushrooms

6 cloves garlic, minced

2 teaspoons minced fresh thyme

¼ teaspoon ground nutmeg

½ cup dry white wine

2 cups Cauliflower Purée (page 72)

¼ cup nutritional yeast

Sea salt and black pepper to taste

1 10-ounce package frozen green peas

12 ounces whole-grain penne pasta, cooked according to package instructions

Drain the porcini mushrooms, reserving ½ cup of the soaking liquid, and chop them up. Set the porcini mushrooms aside.

Sauté the shallot and sliced mushrooms in a large saucepan over medium heat for 7 or 8 minutes. Add water 1 to 2 tablespoons at a time to keep them from sticking. Add the porcini mushrooms, garlic, thyme, and nutmeg, and cook for another minute. Add the wine and the porcini soaking liquid, let simmer until the liquid has almost evaporated, and then add the cauliflower purée, nutritional yeast, and salt and pepper to taste. Add the frozen peas and cook for another minute or two. Toss with the cooked pasta.

Del's Stuffed "Beast"

For me, the baked tofu in this recipe is just a nice way to present my favorite of holiday dishes—the cornbread stuffing. Give me a big bowl of stuffing and some cranberry sauce and I am good to go. There will be stuffing left over from this recipe, so you could make extra tofu and serve even six guests—or you could call me to help you polish it off.

Stuffing

1 medium yellow onion, finely chopped

2 stalks celery, finely chopped

1 teaspoon dried sage

1 teaspoon poultry seasoning

2 cups Cornbread, crumbled (page 258)

2 cups whole-wheat bread crumbs

1 to 1½ cups vegetable stock or Basic Soup Stock (page 146)

Sea salt and black pepper to taste

Baked Tofu (page 232)

In a large sauté pan over medium heat, sauté the onion and celery for 8 to 10 minutes, until the vegetables are tender. Add water 1 to 2 tablespoons at a time to keep them from sticking. Add the sage and poultry seasoning. Combine well and remove from heat. Set aside.

Place the crumbled cornbread and bread crumbs in a large bowl. Add the cooked vegetable mixture, 1 cup of the vegetable stock, and salt and pepper to taste. If the stuffing seems dry, add more vegetable stock. Set aside while you make the tofu.

The Best Mushroom Gravy Ever (pages 98–99) drizzled over Del's Stuffed "Beast."

Baked Tofu

SERVES 4

This recipe is great paired with the cornbread stuffing in Del's Stuffed "Beast," but it also can be used in stir-fries or for sandwiches.

1 pound extra-firm tofu, drained

¼ cup maple syrup

¼ cup Bragg's Liquid Aminos or low-sodium soy sauce

3 cloves garlic, finely minced

1 tablespoon minced fresh ginger

½ teaspoon black pepper

Preheat the oven to 375 degrees F.

Press the tofu for 30 minutes between two towels with a weight on top (a cast-iron skillet works great, but so does a large can of juice). Cut the tofu in half diagonally down through the top to create two triangular pieces, then put the triangles cut side down and cut each piece in half so that you have four triangles, each about 2 inches across. Cut a slit most of the way through the middle of each triangle and stuff each piece with some of the cornbread stuffing. Place the tofu on a shallow nonstick pan and set aside while you prepare the marinade.

Combine the maple syrup, Bragg's Liquid Aminos or soy sauce, garlic, ginger, and pepper in a bowl, and then pour it over the stuffed tofu. Let it sit for 30 minutes, then gently turn each piece over, and let the other side marinate. Bake the stuffed tofu for 35 to 40 minutes, until browned.

Sukiyaki

SERVES 4

Sukiyaki is a Japanese soup or stew usually made with meat, vegetables, and a broth made of soy sauce, mirin (a Japanese rice wine used in cooking), and sugar. I make it with brown rice noodles (though udon or soba are often used). It is one of my favorite noodle dishes and comes together quickly once all the ingredients are assembled. Most of the ingredients for this dish can be found in traditional grocery stores, though I sometimes have to go to my co-op or local natural foods store to find seitan.

8 ounces brown rice spaghetti

1 leek, white part only, washed and thinly sliced on the diagonal

2 cups shiitake mushrooms, stems removed

3 cups mushroom or vegetable stock or Basic Soup Stock (page 146)

1 8-ounce package traditional-style seitan, thinly sliced

2 tablespoons brown rice syrup or agave nectar

¼ cup sake

2 tablespoons mirin

¼ cup plus 2 tablespoons low-sodium soy sauce
   or tamari
1 bunch fresh spinach, coarsely chopped

Cook the pasta according to package instructions. Drain and set aside.

Sauté the leek and mushrooms in a large skillet
over medium-high heat for 5 minutes. Add water 1
to 2 tablespoons at a time to keep the vegetables
from sticking. Add the stock, seitan, syrup or
agave nectar, sake, mirin, and soy sauce to the
vegetables and mix well. Bring the mixture to a
boil and add the spinach and noodles.

Bibimbap (page 237)
Simple Candied Sweet
Potatoes (page 263)

Bibimbap

This most popular of Korean dishes is also one of my favorite dinners. I keep gochujang (a Korean hot pepper paste) on hand and always have cooked rice in the fridge. You can make this dish with whatever vegetables you have, but my favorite version includes steamed spinach and candied sweet potatoes. Other traditional toppings include mung bean sprouts, grated carrots—and, of course, marinated beef and fried egg, but let's not go there.

4 cups cooked brown rice

1 recipe Simple Candied Sweet Potatoes (page 263)

4 cups fresh spinach, steamed until wilted, about 4 to 5 minutes

2 cups mung bean sprouts

2 carrots, grated

Gochujang to taste

To serve, divide the rice between four bowls and arrange the vegetables around and over the rice. Let each person add gochujang sauce to taste. Each person mixes everything in their bowl together and enjoys!

Mushroom Bourguignon

SERVES 4

See photo on pages 260–261.

Beef bourguignon is a traditional French dish of beef braised in red wine. This version made with no added fat is full of flavor from the earthy mushrooms, red wine, and fresh herbs. I eat it over cooked noodles and sometimes as a topping for baked potatoes or Parsnip Mashed Potatoes (page 262).

1 large yellow onion, diced into ½-inch cubes

2 pounds portobello mushroom caps (about 8 cups), cut into 1-inch pieces

2 medium carrots, peeled and diced into ½-inch cubes

4 cloves garlic, minced

2 teaspoons minced fresh thyme

2 teaspoons minced fresh rosemary

1 fresh sage leaf, minced

2 cups dry red wine

2 cups vegetable stock or Basic Soup Stock (page 146)

2 tablespoons tomato paste

1 cup frozen green peas

2 tablespoons arrowroot powder, dissolved in

¼ cup cold water

Sea salt and black pepper to taste

In a large saucepan, sauté the onion over medium heat for 7 to 8 minutes. Add water 1 to 2 tablespoons at a time to keep the onion from sticking. Add the mushrooms and carrots. Cook for 2 minutes. Add the garlic, thyme, rosemary, sage, wine, vegetable stock, and tomato paste. Cover the pan and simmer the stew until the mushrooms are tender, about 20 minutes. Stir in the frozen peas and the arrowroot mixture, and cook for 5 minutes. Remove from heat and add salt and pepper to taste.

Hot and Sour Eggplant Ratatouille

SERVES 4

Serve this over brown rice or eat it in a whole-grain flatbread as a wrap.

2 large eggplants, diced into ½-inch cubes

Sea salt to taste

¼ cup low-sodium soy sauce

3 tablespoons red wine vinegar

¼ cup plus 2 tablespoons Best Date Syrup Ever
   (page 83)

2 jalapeño or other hot chile peppers, diced small

4 teaspoons arrowroot powder

2 medium onions, diced into ½-inch cubes

2 medium red bell peppers, diced into
   ½-inch cubes

4 cups cooked brown rice

Place the cubed eggplants in a large bowl and sprinkle with salt. Let it sit for 30 minutes. Rinse well and drain on paper towels.

Combine the soy sauce, vinegar, date syrup, jalapeño peppers, and arrowroot powder in a small bowl and set it aside.

Heat a large skillet over medium-high heat. Add the onions, red bell peppers, and eggplants, and sauté for 8 to 10 minutes, until the eggplants are tender. Add water 1 to 2 tablespoons at a time to keep the vegetables from sticking. Add the sauce and cook until it thickens, about 2 minutes. Serve over the brown rice.

10

Side Dishes

Balsamic-Glazed Brussels Sprouts

Brussels sprouts are one of my favorite vegetables. I eat them steamed and seasoned with salt, pepper, and nutritional yeast, or, as in this recipe, glazed with balsamic vinegar.

> 1½ pounds brussels sprouts (about 6 cups),
>   trimmed and halved
> 1 large yellow onion, diced
> 1 cup balsamic vinegar, reduced to ½ cup (see note)
> ¼ cup brown rice syrup
> Sea salt and black pepper to taste

Steam the brussels sprouts until tender, about 10 minutes. While they steam, sauté the onion in a large skillet over medium heat for 10 minutes, until it is well browned. Add water 1 to 2 tablespoons at a time to keep them from sticking. Add the steamed brussels sprouts, balsamic vinegar reduction, and syrup, and mix well. Cook for 3 to 4 minutes. Season with salt and pepper.

Chef's Note · To reduce the balsamic vinegar, place it in a small saucepan over medium heat and cook it until it is reduced to ½ cup.

Eat Your Greens

My mom often made a big pot of greens—some-times collard, sometimes mustard, or sometimes a combination of greens. Cooking times for greens depend on the type of greens you are cooking and the maturity of the greens. Collard and turnip greens take longer—about 40 to 50 minutes; kale and mustard greens take about 15 minutes; and spinach and arugula, just a few minutes.

1 large onion, diced

3 cloves garlic, minced

2 pounds collard or turnip greens, stemmed
   and washed

4 cups vegetable stock or Basic Soup Stock
   (page 146)

2 teaspoons mellow white miso

Sea salt and black pepper to taste

Sauté the onion in a large pot over medium heat for 4 to 5 minutes, until it starts to brown. Add water 1 to 2 tablespoons at a time to keep the onion from sticking. Add the garlic and cook for another minute. Add the greens and vegetable stock, decrease the heat to low, cover, and allow to simmer gently for 45 minutes, until the greens are tender. Stir the greens once as they cook. Remove ½ cup of the vegetable stock from the pot and add it to a bowl with the miso. Whisk the mixture until smooth and creamy, and then add it to the pot with the greens. Season with pepper and mix well. Add salt to taste and serve.

Chef's Note • If you want to use a mixture of greens, add the longer-cooking greens first and then the quicker-cooking greens about halfway through.

Mustard Greens

I often make a pot of greens to have on hand. Frequently they end up in a bowl over rice and beans, served with hot pepper or a little nutritional yeast.

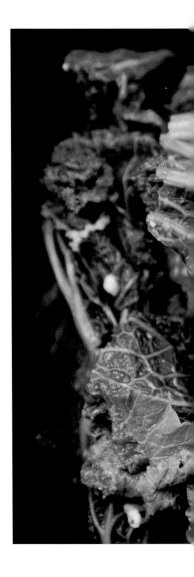

4 pounds mustard greens, stemmed and washed
1 large onion, diced
2 cloves garlic, minced
Sea salt and black pepper to taste

Bring a large pot of water to a boil, add the mustard greens in batches, and let them cook for 5 minutes. Remove the greens from the water and transfer them to a large bowl with ice water to stop their cooking and help them retain their color.

Sauté the onion in a large skillet for 7 to 8 minutes over medium heat. Add water 1 to 2 tablespoons at a time to keep the onion from sticking. Add the garlic and cook for another minute. Add the greens and cook for 5 minutes. Season with salt and pepper.

Chef's Note • If you want to make this dish with quick-cooking arugula or spinach, skip the part where you cook the greens in boiling water. Instead, cook them, covered, with the sautéed onion and garlic for a few minutes and then season with salt and pepper.

Tangy BBQ Baked Beans (page 251)
Potato Salad (page 252)
Black Bean Burger (page 204)
Jalapeño Mayonnaise (page 86)

Tangy BBQ Baked Beans

SERVES 4

You control the flavor and spice in these simple baked beans by choosing your favorite bottle of barbecue sauce. Canned pinto beans (navy or great northern beans work well, too) make these a breeze to prepare. For an extra kick, toss some sliced jalapeño peppers or red pepper flakes into the sauce while cooking, or add a can of sliced pineapple for a luau flair.

½ cup ketchup
¾ cup barbecue sauce
½ cup water
1 tablespoon Bragg's Liquid Aminos
2 tablespoons maple syrup
1 tablespoon mustard
3 cups canned pinto beans, drained and rinsed
Sea salt to taste

Preheat the oven to 325 degrees F.

Mix the ketchup, barbecue sauce, water, Bragg's Liquid Aminos, syrup, and mustard together in a saucepan. Bring to a boil. Decrease heat and simmer for 5 minutes. Add the beans, and salt to taste. Transfer to a casserole dish and bake, uncovered, for 1 hour.

Potato Salad

See photo on page 250.

Here is my go-to summer picnic potluck dish. Sometimes just to shake things up I add olives and capers and plenty of fresh dill.

> 6 medium potatoes (I like red skin or Yukon gold)
> ¾ cup Low-Fat Mayonnaise (page 84)
> ¼ cup Dijon mustard
> 2 tablespoons brown rice vinegar
> ½ medium yellow onion, chopped
> 2 stalks celery, diced
> Sea salt and black pepper to taste

Dice potatoes into ½-inch cubes. Place them in a large pot with boiling water to cover. Boil them for 12 to 15 minutes, until they're tender. Do not overcook them or they will become mushy. Remove from heat, drain the potatoes, and rinse them under cold water until cool. Drain and add remaining ingredients. Chill well before serving.

Coleslaw

SERVES 8

Another summer favorite gets a healthy makeover.
By using the already prepared coleslaw mix you
can have this recipe prepared in about 15 minutes.
Ready, set, go!!!

1 cup Low-Fat Mayonnaise (page 84)

¼ cup brown rice vinegar

2 teaspoons Dijon mustard

2 tablespoons brown rice syrup

1 16-ounce package coleslaw mix

½ small red onion, diced small

2 tablespoons finely chopped fresh tarragon

In a small bowl, whisk together the mayonnaise,
vinegar, mustard, and syrup. Place the coleslaw
mix in a large bowl and add the dressing, red
onion, and tarragon. Mix well. Refrigerate for
1 hour before serving.

(continued on following page)

(continued from previous page)

Spicy Asian Slaw

1 red bell pepper, diced small

1 cup chopped fresh cilantro

6 green onions, chopped

2 tablespoons minced fresh ginger

3 cloves garlic, minced

1 jalapeño pepper, minced (optional)

Add all ingredients to the preceding standard coleslaw recipe above for a slaw with a kick, and serve it on the side with Black Bean Burgers (page 204).

Cilantro-Lime Slaw

I love this slaw with Adzuki Bean Tacos
(page 216). The tangy, spicy slaw contrasts nicely
with the almost-sweet adzuki beans in the tacos.

4 cups coleslaw mix

½ cup chopped fresh cilantro

1 jalapeño pepper, minced (optional)

Zest and juice of 1 lime

4 tablespoons brown rice vinegar, or use more or
  less to taste

Sea salt to taste

Combine all ingredients in a bowl and mix well.

Jicama Slaw with Creamy Poppy Seed Dressing

Crisp, clean-tasting jicama gets dressed up with this delicious poppy seed dressing. This slaw makes a great filling for wraps with hummus.

- 2 tablespoons agave nectar or brown rice syrup
- 2 tablespoons rice wine vinegar
- 1 tablespoon poppy seeds
- ½ tablespoon Dijon mustard
- ½ teaspoon onion powder
- ¼ teaspoon sea salt
- ¾ cup firm silken tofu (about ½ of a 12-ounce package)
- 6 cups grated jicama
- 1 medium carrot, grated
- 6 green onions, thinly sliced

To make the dressing, combine the agave nectar or brown rice syrup, rice wine vinegar, poppy seeds, Dijon mustard, onion powder, salt, and silken tofu in a food processor or a blender, and purée until smooth and creamy.

Add the remaining ingredients to a bowl with the dressing; mix well. Refrigerate until ready to serve.

Cornbread

SERVES 8

I love cornbread with soup or chili for lunch or dinner, or even with some apple butter on it for a quick breakfast. Applesauce is a good substitute for eggs and oil in baking and you won't taste it.

- 1½ cups whole-wheat pastry flour
- 1½ cups cornmeal
- 4 teaspoons baking powder
- ½ teaspoon sea salt
- 2 tablespoons Best Date Syrup Ever (page 83)
- ½ cup unsweetened applesauce
- 2 cups unsweetened almond milk

Preheat the oven to 350 degrees F. In a medium bowl, combine the flour, cornmeal, baking powder, and salt. Make a well in the center of the flour mixture by scooping the flour to the side of the bowl with a spoon, and add the date syrup, applesauce, and almond milk to the well. Then gently fold the liquid mixture into the flour mixture. Spoon the batter into an 8 × 8 inch square nonstick baking dish and bake for 30 to 35 minutes, until a toothpick inserted in the center of the pan comes out clean. Let cool before serving.

Cornbread (page 258)
Creole Corn Chowder
(page 147)

Cornbread (page 258)
Creole Corn Chowder
(page 147)

VARIATION

Blueberry-Cornbread Muffins

Add ½ pint of fresh blueberries to the batter and
bake in nonstick muffin tins for 25 to 30 minutes
for a nice treat.

Parsnip Mashed Potatoes (page 262)
Mushroom Bourguignon (page 238)

Parsnip Mashed Potatoes

SERVES 4

See photo on pages 260–261.

Parsnips add a little zing to otherwise-ordinary mashed potatoes. They also make them a little creamier. While I normally pass over mashed potatoes as a side dish, I can eat a bowlful of this tasty version.

6 medium red or white new potatoes, cubed
3 medium parsnips, peeled and cubed
Dash of cayenne pepper
1 teaspoon sea salt

Put the potatoes and parsnips in a large pot with just enough water to cover the vegetables. Bring to a boil, decrease heat to medium, and then cover and simmer for 20 to 30 minutes, stirring occasionally with a spoon. Test the tenderness of the potatoes and parsnips with a fork; they should pierce easily and be tender yet firm. Drain any remaining liquid and mash the potatoes and parsnips with a potato masher until there are no visible lumps. Gently stir in the cayenne pepper and salt with a wooden spoon.

Simple Candied Sweet Potatoes

SERVES 4

See photo on page 236.

Most candied sweet potato recipes are chock-full of butter, sugar, and probably marshmallows. This one that I eat with my favorite Korean dish, Bibimbap (page 237), has just three ingredients and comes together quickly. I keep Best Date Syrup Ever on hand so I always have a healthy sweetener when I want something sweet besides fresh fruit.

3 cups sweet potatoes, peeled and diced into
   ½-inch cubes
¾ cup Best Date Syrup Ever (page 83)
Black sesame seeds (garnish)

Steam the sweet potatoes for 8 to 10 minutes, until tender. While they steam, add the date syrup to a large skillet with ¼ cup water and bring it to a boil. Let it simmer for 5 minutes. Add the steamed sweet potatoes and let them cook for another minute. Serve garnished with the black sesame seeds.

Fig Deltons (page 274)

11

Desserts

I eat dessert rarely. Even though the dessert recipes that follow are healthier than most you'll find—they are lower in sugar, include whole grains, and have no added oil—they can still be full of concentrated calories and are best saved for birthdays and truly special occasions.

Very Berry Ice Cream

I used to eat a pint of ice cream in a single sitting and then spend the rest of the day sleeping
off the resulting "hangover." Get rid of the fat and
sugar and voilà—no hangover. Make this delicious
ice "cream" with any berries and try the flavoring
options that follow for some added oomph. Keep
frozen berries and frozen bananas on hand and you
have an instant treat.

3 bananas, sliced
1 cup frozen berries
¾ to 1 cup unsweetened almond milk,
    well chilled
¼ teaspoon stevia powder
Zest of 1 lemon

Place the sliced bananas on a baking sheet and
place in the freezer until hard, about 2 hours.
Combine the frozen bananas, frozen berries,
¾ cup almond milk, stevia powder, and lemon
zest in a blender and purée until smooth and
creamy. Add more almond milk if necessary to
make a creamy consistency. Serve immediately.

Vanilla Ice Cream

Replace the berries with 2 additional frozen bananas, eliminate the lemon zest, and add ¼ teaspoon vanilla extract for a vanilla-flavored ice cream.

Chocolate Ice Cream

Replace the berries with 2 additional frozen bananas, eliminate the lemon zest, and add ¼ teaspoon vanilla extract and 2 teaspoons unsweetened cocoa powder for a chocolate-flavored ice cream.

Lemon-Berry Sorbet

If you can find fresh, in-season berries at the farmers' market, buy a lot of them, then freeze what you don't eat, and have them handy for tasty treats like this one.

1 quart frozen berries

1 ripe banana, sliced and frozen

½ tablespoon stevia extract, or use more or less to taste

¼ cup fresh lemon juice

½ teaspoon lemon zest

2 tablespoons vodka

Place the berries and banana slices in a food processor and pulse until they are the size of peas. Add the stevia extract, lemon juice and zest, and vodka, and purée until smooth. Place the mixture into a shallow dish and freeze for 2 to 3 hours, stirring every 30 minutes or so until firm.

Chef's Note • I add a banana and a little vodka to this recipe to make the sorbet less icy, but you can leave both out if you prefer. You can also make this dish in your ice cream maker for a smoother texture.

Sweet Potato–
Brown Rice Pudding

SERVES 6

One of my favorite desserts is sweet potato pie.
I used to make it for my personal chef service,
sell one piece, and, over the course of the day,
eat the rest of the pie myself. Now when I crave
sweet potato pie, I make this delicious rice pudding
instead. It has all the flavor of my favorite pie without the added fat or sugar.

> 4 cups unsweetened almond milk
> ¾ cup Best Date Syrup Ever (page 83), or use
>   more or less to taste
> 2 teaspoons pure vanilla extract
> Zest of 1 orange
> 2 teaspoons ground cinnamon
> ½ teaspoon allspice
> ½ teaspoon ground ginger
> 3 cups cooked short-grain brown rice
> 2 cups sweet potato purée

Add the almond milk, date syrup, vanilla, orange zest, and spices to a saucepan. Simmer the mixture over medium heat for 5 minutes. Stir in the cooked rice and cook, covered, for 20 minutes, stirring occasionally. Add the sweet potato purée and cook for 10 minutes more, stirring frequently to keep the mixture from sticking.

Chocolate Pudding

Guilt-free chocolate pudding makes me very happy, and this one is an excellent dish to share with someone you really, really like.

1 12-ounce package lite silken tofu, drained

⅓ cup unsweetened cocoa powder

1 cup Best Date Syrup Ever (page 83), or use more or less to taste

2–½ teaspoon vanilla extract

Pinch of sea salt

Combine all ingredients in a blender and purée until smooth and creamy. Refrigerate until well chilled.

Fig Deltons

See photo on pages 264–265.

I love Fig Newtons, and even though you can get them fat-free, they are still high in sugar. Here is my low-fat and sugar-free version.

Filling

1 pound dried figs (about 3 cups), stemmed and chopped

¾ cup Best Date Syrup Ever (page 83)

Zest of 1 orange

Crust and Topping

1 cup whole-wheat pastry flour

1 cup barley flour

½ tablespoon baking powder

1 teaspoon ground cinnamon

¼ teaspoon sea salt

1 cup Best Date Syrup Ever (page 83)

¾ cup applesauce

1 teaspoon vanilla extract

Preheat the oven to 350 degrees F. Line an 8 × 8 inch square baking pan with parchment paper and set aside.

To make the filling, purée the figs with the date syrup and orange zest in a food processor until smooth and creamy. Add water as needed to make a smooth consistency. Set aside.

To make the batter for the crust and topping, combine the flours, baking powder, cinnamon, and salt in a bowl and mix well. Add the date syrup, applesauce, and vanilla extract to another bowl and mix. Add the applesauce mixture to the bowl with the flour mixture and gently fold the ingredients together.

To assemble the bars:

Spread half of the batter in the prepared pan. Spread the fig filling over it and spread the remaining batter on top of the filling. Bake for 20 to 25 minutes, until a toothpick inserted in the center of the pan comes out clean. Let cool before cutting into squares.

Pineapple Sherbet

SERVES 4

My grandmother Florence was a fan of sherbet and we had it often for dessert. Pineapple sherbet is my favorite, and here is my very healthy version of a family favorite.

3 bananas, sliced

1½ cups chopped pineapple

¾ to 1 cup unsweetened almond milk, well chilled

¼ teaspoon stevia powder

Zest of 1 lemon

Place the sliced bananas on a baking sheet and freeze until hard, about 2 hours. Place the chopped pineapple on a separate baking sheet and freeze until hard, about 2 hours.

Combine the bananas, ¾ cup almond milk, stevia powder, and lemon zest in a food processor and purée until smooth and creamy. Add more almond milk if needed to make a creamy consistency. Add the frozen pineapple and pulse-chop to incorporate well. Serve immediately.

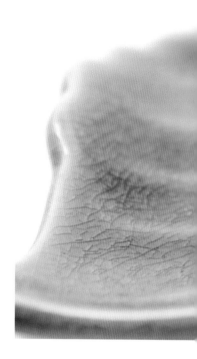

Index

279

Ingredients
    food labels, 44–45, 47–48
    pantry staples, 52–54
    refrigerated/frozen foods, 54–55
    seasonings, 53–54, 63, 64–67
    selecting, 63

J

Jalapeño Mayonnaise, 86, *250*
Jicama Slaw with Creamy Poppy Seed
    Dressing, 256–257, *257*

K

Kalamata-Lemon Hummus, 132
King Avenue Coffeehouse, 10–11
Kiwis, in Breakfast Pizza, Big Fat, *114*, 115
Knives, 52
Kombu, 57

L

Leek Sauce, Creamy, *78*, 79
Lemon
   -Berry Sorbet, *268*, 269
   -Kalamata Hummus, 132
Lentil Soup, Red, Turkish, 160–161, *161*
Lime-Cilantro Slaw, 255
Low-fat diet. *See* Plant-based, low-fat diet

M

Mango
    in "Chicken" Salad, Tropical, *200*, 201
   -Ginger Smoothie, *102*, 104
    Salad Dressing, *96*, 97
Maple
   -Banana Granola, 106, *107*
    Cream, 87, *107*
Mayonnaise
    Jalapeño, 86, *250*
    Low-Fat, 84, *85*
Melon, in White Gazpacho, 150, *151*
Milks, plant, 53, 58
Mirepoix, 62

Miso-Ginger Dressing, *89*, 95
Miso paste, 54
Mr. Benedict, 122–125, *123*
Muffins, Blueberry-Cornbread, 259
Mushroom(s)
    Bourguignon, 238–239, *260–261*
    in Breakfast Casserole, Del's Big,
      118–119, *120–121*
    Burritos, Breakfast, 116–117, *117*
    Flatbread, Sun-Dried Tomato Pesto,
      190–191, *191*
    Gravy, The Best Gravy Ever, 98,
      99, 100
    Penne with Peas and, 228–229, *229*
    Portobello Wraps with Spicy Asian Slaw,
      177–178, *179*
    Soup, Cream of, 156–157, *158–159*
    in Sukiyaki, 234–235
    Tacos with Chipotle Cream, 208–209
Mustard Greens, 248, *249*

N

Noodles
    Bangkok, 218–219, *219*
    in Sukiyaki, 234–235
Nutrition, Five Laws of, 12–22
Nutrition labels, 45, 47–50

O

Oatmeal
    Basic, 111
    in Granola, Banana-Maple, 106, *107*
    with Rhubarb, Poached, 112, *113*
Oil-free cooking, 20–22, 58
Olives, Kalamata-Lemon Hummus, 132
Onions
    Red, Pickled, 196–197
    seasoning with, 65, 66
    sulfides in, 32, 33–34

P

Pantry staples, 52–54
Parsnip Mashed Potatoes, *260–261*, 262

Spice(s)
  Creole Spice Blend, 149
  and Fruit Breakfast Bars, *108*, 109–110
  pantry staples, 53–54
  seasoning with, 63, 64–67
Spicy Asian Slaw, 254
Spicy Black Bean–Sweet Potato Stew,
    164–165
Spicy Seitan, 125
Spinach
  -Artichoke Dip, *140*, 141
  in Bangkok Noodles, 218–219, *219*
  Bibimbap, *236*, 237
  "Ricotta," 124
  "Ricotta," in Mr. Benedict, 122–123, *123*
  in Sukiyaki, 234–235
  -Wasabi Hummus, 129
Spreads. *See* Dips and Spreads; Hummus
Squash
  Curried Squash Sauce, Pasta with, *224*,
    224–225
  Enchiladas, Three Sisters, 214–215, *215*
  White Bean Veggie Wrap, 181, *182–183*
Sroufe, Del
  family dietary history of, 4–7
  health of, 15–17
  life restrictions of weight on, 9–10
  nutrition laws of, 12–22
  off-limits subject of weight, 7–9
  and vegan bakery lifestyle, 11–14
  vegan high caloric diet of, 3–4, 14
  vegetarianism of, 10–11
  and Wellness Forum, 17–18, 20
Stew
  Black Bean–Sweet Potato, Spicy, 164–165
  Sukiyaki, 234–235
Stir-frying, without oil, 61, 64
Stock, Soup, Basic, 146
Strawberries, in Breakfast Pizza, Big Fat,
    114, 115
Stuffed "Beast," Del's, *99*, 230–231, *231*
Substitutions, recipe, 56–58
Succotash Soup, 162–163, *163*
Sugars, concentrated, 29–30
Sukiyaki, 234–235
Sulfides, 32, 33–34

Sun-Dried Tomato Pesto Flatbread,
    190–191, *191*
Sweeteners, 29, 45, 54
Sweet Potato(es)
  Bisque, Chilled, 154–155
  –Black Bean Enchiladas, 210–211, *212–213*
  –Black Bean Stew, Spicy, 164–165
  -Brown Rice Pudding, 270–271, *271*
  Candied, in Bibimbap, *236*, 237
  Candied, Simple, *236*, 263
  Gado Gado, 202–203, *203*
Syrup, The Best Date Syrup Ever, *82–83*, 83

T

Tacos
  Adzuki Bean, 216–217, *217*
  Mushroom, with Chipotle Cream, 208–
    209
Tempeh, 55, 56
Thousand Island Dressing, *89*, 94
Three Sisters Enchiladas, 214–215, *215*
Tofu
  Baked, 232–233
  Breakfast Casserole, Del's Big, 118–119,
    120–121
  lightly processed, 29
  Scramble, in Breakfast Burritos,
    116–117, *117*
  storage of, 54–55
  Stuffed "Beast," Del's, *99*, 230–231, *231*
  substitutions, 56, 57
Tofu, Silken, 54, 57
  Breakfast Casserole, Del's Big, 118–119,
    120–121
  Chocolate Pudding, *272*, 273
  Hollandaise Sauce, 77
  Maple Cream, 87, *107*
  Mayonnaise, Low-Fat, 84, *85*
  Poppy Seed Dressing, Creamy, Jicama
    Slaw with, 256–257, *257*
  Spinach "Ricotta," 124
Tomato(es)
  Bisque, Chilled, *152*, 153
  Flatbread, Sun-Dried Tomato Pesto,
    190–191, *191*

Flatbread, Hummus, Pesto and, *192*, 193
as pantry staple, 52
Pizza, Red, White, and Green, 188, *189*
Sauce, Garden Fresh, 80, *81*
Tortillas
Burritos, Black Bean, 180
Burritos, Breakfast, 116–117, *117*
Enchiladas, Sweet Potato–Black Bean,
210–211, *212–213*
Enchiladas, Three Sisters, 214–215, *215*
Tacos, Adzuki Bean, 216–217, *217*
Tacos, Mushroom, with Chipotle Cream,
208–209
Wraps, Portobello, with Spicy Asian Slaw,
177–178, *179*
Wraps, Zucchini Pritti–Hummus, *174*,
175–176
Tropical "Chicken" Salad, *200*, 201
Turkish Red Lentil Soup, 160–161, *161*
Turnips Greens, Eat Your, 246–247, *247*

U

United States Department of Agriculture
(USDA), 37

V

Vanilla Ice Cream, 267
Vegan diet. *See also* Plant-based, low-fat
diet
Atkins, 14–15
high caloric foods in, 3–4, 14, 37–38,
39–40
Vegetables. *See also specific vegetables*
baking/roasting, 61–62
braising, 61
frozen, 55
Gado Gado, 202–203, *203*
pantry staples, 52
Pasta, Summer, with Veggies and
"Cream," 220–221, *221*
phytochemicals in, 32–35
sautéing, 58, 60–61
Soup Stock, Basic, 146
starchy, 40–42

stewing, 62
stir-frying, 61
Very Berry Ice Cream, 266, *267*
Vinaigrette, Creamy Dijon, 88, *89*

W

Wasabi-Spinach Hummus, 129
Watercress-Potato Soup, 168, *169*
Water intake, 31, 44
Weight, 3–4, 7
Weight loss, 7, 14–15, 41–43, 62
Wellness Forum, 17–18, 20
White Bean(s)
in Cucumber Dressing, *90*, 91
Pesto, 138, *139*
Pesto, Hot and Sour Ratatouille
Calzones with, *184*, 185
Spread, 134
Spread, Chestnut and, 135, *136–137*
Veggie Wrap, 181, *182–183*
White Gazpacho, 150, *151*
Whole-grain foods, 41
Whole-Wheat Pizza Dough, 186–187
Wraps
Portobello, with Spicy Asian Slaw,
177–178, *179*
White Bean Veggie, 181, *182–183*
Zucchini Pritti–Hummus, *174*, 175–176

Y

Yo-yo dieting, 15

Z

Zucchini
Pasta, Summer, with Veggies and
"Cream," 220–221, *221*
Pizza, Red, White, and Green, 188, *189*
Pritti–Hummus Wrap, *174*, 175–176
Sun-Dried Tomato Pesto Flatbread,
190–191, *191*

Acknowledgments

Many, many thanks go out to my friend and mentor Dr. Pam Popper for her patience and perseverance as she worked harder sometimes than I did to help me take control of my weight and my health. Thank you to Glen Merzer for helping me to tell my story. Thank you to an army of recipe testers for your willingness to be critical; to Glenn Yeffeth and the staff at BenBella Books: Leigh Camp, Jennifer Canzoneri, Debbie Harmsen, Adrienne Lang, Monica Lowry, Lindsay Marshall, and Vy Tran; to Nicole Schlosser and Shannon Kelly for the excellent copyediting; to Robert Metzger for being a meticulous photographer—and food stylist; to Adam Koch for exceptional additional photography; and to Elizabeth and Jimmy for years of faith, support, and friendship.

Glen Merzer adds special thanks to his friend Dr. John Tanner for the inspiration.

About the Authors

Del Sroufe has worked in vegan and vegetarian kitchens for more than twenty-three years, most recently as chef and co-owner of Wellness Forum Foods, a plant-based meal delivery and catering service that emphasizes healthy, minimally processed foods. He teaches cooking classes and is the lead author of the bestselling cookbook *Forks Over Knives: The Cookbook*. He has also contributed recipes to *Food Over Medicine,* by Dr. Pam Popper and Glen Merzer.

Glen Merzer is coauthor with Dr. Pam Popper of *Food Over Medicine*, with Howard Lyman of *Mad Cowboy: Plain Truth from the Cattle Rancher Who Won't Eat Meat*, and with Howard Lyman and Joanna Samorow-Merzer of *No More Bull!: The Mad Cowboy Targets America's Worst Enemy: Our Diet*. He also coauthored Chef AJ's *Unprocessed* and is currently editing the forthcoming *HappyCow Cookbook.* Glen is a playwright and screenwriter living in Los Angeles. He has been a vegetarian for forty years and a vegan for the last twenty.